Foreword

The author, Professor Jack Simmons, has been associated with the National Railway Museum since its beginning and has since 1969 been a member of the Advisory Council of its parent body, the Science Museum. So he and I have worked together for quite a long time.

We share an enthusiasm for museums, and, in particular, a strong affection for the National Railway Museum. Nor are we alone in this, for first the North of England, then the whole country and beyond took to this new venture and were fascinated by its displays, which are eye-catching and romantic, and anything but static.

Now the Museum is five years old and its collection is further enlarged and more broadly-based. Already it has had an extension to its main building to cope with its many visitors and more land and another building have been obtained for its behind-the-scenes activity. What we are trying to do is to make sure that this national museum, so well located in York, has a splendid life of its own and that it is as healthy in twenty or fifty years' time as it is now.

Jack Simmons and his fellow members of the NRM Committee have all been greatly involved in this, and I certainly think that it is this involvement and his regard for the Museum, coupled with the fact that he is a notable historian of technology, that led him to write this book. I am very glad that he has done so, and hope that you enjoy it as much as I have.

MARGARET WESTON

Director Science Museum, London
National Railway Museum, York
October 1980

Da

The

RAL

Please renew/return this item by the last date shown.

So that your telephone call is charged at local rate, please call the numbers as set out below:

	From Area codes 01923 or 020:	From the rest of Herts:
Renewals:	01923 471373	01438 737373
Enquiries:	01923 471333	01438 737333
Textphone:	01923 471599	01438 737599

L32   www.hertsdirect.org/librarycatalogue

LONDON HER MAJESTY'S STATIONERY OFFICE

ISBN 0 11 290299 9

Preface

The National Railway Museum was opened at York in 1975. Few museums can be said to be the product of a single enterprise, in forming their collections and housing them. Nearly all have evolved from many years' work, from the efforts of several individuals or groups of people devoted to the subjects they touch, collectors and enthusiasts, administrators and public persons. No museum exemplifies that more clearly than this one, which is the product of more than fifty years' discussion and argument (sometimes heated), and of unending patience. To appreciate the achievement it represents, all these things must be understood and borne in mind.

This book starts therefore with the growth of the idea of such a museum in Britain, from its initial airing in the Victorian age to the establishment of the first railway museum at York and then, in the 1960s, of those at Clapham and Swindon; going on to sketch the discussion that arose over the setting-up of a National Railway Museum at York. This is the background against which the Museum has to be seen: the Museum itself, fully open now to visitors, and attracting them from all over the world–$7\frac{3}{4}$ million of them already by September 1980.

The central part of this book, and the largest one, is given to a descriptive account of that display, of what the visitor can see. But a museum's public display represents only one element of its work. The last section turns to examine something of what he does not see, the work the Museum is constantly engaged on out of the public eye: its activities in education, in the care and maintenance of the collections, in aiding the railway preservation movement and in promoting research. When all these things are taken into account as well as the public display, the Museum can be appreciated for what it is: a truly national institution.

This book is not a catalogue, or a comprehensive guide to the Museum, and for that there are two reasons. This is a large museum. More than 2000 objects are displayed in it, and many more are in its care but not at present shown. They could not all be listed, let alone described in a short book. I have not discussed one of them in any detail. The descriptions provided in the Museum–especially of the locomotives and carriages – are in general full and of a very high standard. The visitor should move on at once to them from what I have to say.

It must also be understood that, for reasons explained elsewhere (pp. 5–6), some objects move in and out of the Museum. Those that are mentioned here were nearly all on display when these words were written. Some of them may have been taken away by the time the book is published, and new ones will then have arrived in their place.

Finally I must explain that although this is an official publication, I have been left free to express opinions, to point out gaps in the collection and other deficiencies, here and there to criticise what has been done. My respect and affection for the whole achievement that the Museum represents will, I hope, be plain.

Leicester   J.S.
5 October 1980

ACKNOWLEDGEMENTS

The author is much indebted to those who have read the text in draft and supplied information to him, especially to the Director of the Science Museum, Dame Margaret Weston, and her predecessor Sir David Follett; to Brian Lacey and John van Riemsdijk; to Dr John Coiley and Peter Semmens, Keeper and Assistant Keeper of the National Railway Museum. He is also grateful to David Eatwell for providing the photographs reproduced as Plates 5 and 6.

Contents

I
The Museum and its setting

The mechanically-operated railway was first developed in Britain. There were two essential elements in its technology: the metal track, strong enough to bear constant and heavy traffic, and the steam locomotive, running upon it. Both of them made their first appearance in Britain, one in the eighteenth century, the other at the beginning of the nineteenth. Both were quickly taken further and improved, first in this country, then elsewhere in Europe and in America. The railway spread all over the world, to become a great instrument of economic and social change. If Englishmen had not developed it first, no doubt others would have done so - Frenchmen perhaps or Americans. But they did, and the fact stands beyond argument. The railway was one of Britain's chief gifts to the world.

Towards the end of the nineteenth century, when people began to look back and assess the extraordinary changes that had come about since its beginning, some of them felt they ought to be commemorated. The railway evidently represented one of those changes, and in several countries railway museums were established, to contain relics of past history: the first two of them, open to the public, at Hamar in Norway in 1897 and at Nuremberg in Germany in 1899. There was some talk for a little while of doing the same thing in Britain, both in the 1890s and again in 1908, but nothing came of it at that time.

The idea was first realised through the energy and enthusiasm of a small group of men on the North Eastern Railway, led by J.B.Harper. When it became certain that the North Eastern Company would lose its identity through being merged into a larger group, under the Railways Act of 1921, these men set themselves to collect relics, which were stored in the basement of the Company's offices at York. The celebration of the centenary of the Stockton & Darlington Railway in 1925 generated a strong interest in the history of railways in Britain, and the larger London & North Eastern Company (of which the North Eastern now formed part) decided to open a public museum, into which these stored relics and others could be moved. For this purpose it allocated the locomotive erecting and repair shops of the old York & North Midland Railway in Queen Street, York. There the first railway museum in Britain was opened in 1927 (Plate 1).

It was small and it soon grew crowded. The Curator, E.M.Bywell, and a number of other people who took an interest in it secured a steady enlargement of its collections, which can be followed through the successive editions of its *Catalogue* from 1933 onwards. By the time the last of them appeared, in 1956, the building was full to overflowing.

It still remained the only British museum devoted solely to the railway. Why should the country have recognised so tardily the importance of preserving the relics of this development, which it had pioneered, and of displaying them? Two explanations may be suggested.

In the first place, in those countries where railway museums had been set up early, the railways – all or most of them – had been nationalised, and it was much easier for a single corporation to take this step than for competing private companies. None of the other three large companies in Britain showed any eagerness to place relics of its own in the custody of the London & North Eastern at York, though eventually three locomotives, one representing each of them, found their way there: *Gladstone*, *Columbine*, and *City of Truro*. Those companies did show some interest in their history, in different ways. The Great Western assembled a valuable collection of small objects, mounted privately in a long corridor at Paddington station. The London Midland & Scottish kept a few treasures at Euston. Both the Great Western and the Southern Companies commissioned histories of their own, based in part upon their records. But these were the result of private decisions, and they did not mean yielding up any of the companies' possessions.

Secondly, it must be remembered that there was already one most important collection of railway relics to be seen in Britain, at the Science Museum in London, a collection with a long history behind it, superior to any other in a national museum in Europe. The Royal Scottish Museum in Edinburgh had another, on a smaller scale; and there were notable railway exhibits elsewhere, for example in museums at Newcastle, Liverpool, and Hull. So the railway was by no means neglected. What it lacked, however, was a comprehensive treatment to portray the vital contribution it made to the growth of the nation in the nineteenth century.

When the railways were nationalised in 1947 a new challenge arose, and a new chance. Twenty-five years earlier the men of the North Eastern Company had shown their loyalty to its memory. Now all the old private companies were disappearing, except a small number of very minor ones; loyalties were strong again and widespread throughout the island, from Scotland to Kent. One of the things that stands greatly to the credit of the new British Transport Commission, set up to manage the nationalised undertaking, is the responsibility it assumed towards the materials of the history of the private companies. It appointed a committee to examine the problems involved in their preservation, which reported in 1950. This led to the setting up of a record office in London, near Paddington station, to accommodate the railways' archives and make them available for public use. At the same time the Commission established a Department of Historical Relics charged with their preservation. It had inherited the Railway Museum at York, and kept it open. But the building was full, and the site too small to permit any large extension. An additional museum was evidently needed, and that was presently provided in London by the opening of the new Museum of British Transport at Clapham, with John H. Scholes as Curator, in 1961–3 (Plate 2). At the same time the Commission entered into an arrangement with the Corporation of Swindon for the establishment of a museum there devoted entirely to the Great Western Railway; and in Scotland a Museum of Transport was set up at Glasgow, which included a strong railway section.

These museums gave Great Britain much of what it needed, but not enough. This was a time of rapid technological change on the British railways, following on the Modernisation Plan of 1955, with the phasing-out of the steam locomotive, the closing of many secondary and branch lines, the introduction of entirely new methods of handling freight; a time when many of the older pieces of equipment, large and small, cried out to be preserved, if they were not to be immediately destroyed. But where should they be preserved, and who should do it? The new museum at Clapham quickly became as full as the old one at York. What was wanted, quite plainly, was a comprehensive national museum of railways, worthy of the country that had done most to evolve them in the past.

Much discussion arose about the proper location of a museum of the kind. Should it be in London, or outside? In the end the Government determined to relieve the British Railways Board (the British Transport Commission's successor) of the responsibility, and to set up a new museum as a branch of the Science Museum. It was to be accommodated, however, not in London but at York. The original museum there was to be replaced by another, in a different building and on a site capable of development, and to be called the National Railway Museum.

There were good reasons in favour of the choice of York. Not only was there a suitable building available there, and a railway museum already in existence, whose collections were internationally known. More than that: York had its own place in the history of railways. It was one of three historic English cathedral cities – the others were Peterborough and Carlisle – that became important centres of the railway industry; and of those three it was the biggest. It was George Hudson's town, the base from which he built up his railway empire in the 1840s, and on that foundation it came to be the meeting-point of seven lines, from London, Sheffield, Leeds, Harrogate, Newcastle, Scarborough, and Hull. When the North Eastern Railway Company emerged by amalgamation in 1854, to comprise one of the largest in Britain, York became its administrative headquarters. The station was rebuilt into its present impressive form in 1871–7, and it was then one of the biggest in Europe. Large railway works were established close by for the building and repair of locomotives and rolling stock. In 1900, taking the employees and their families together, about a fifth of the entire population of the city depended on railway work. That is no longer true today, but York is the headquarters of one of the five Regions of British Railways and one of the busiest junctions on the whole system. The city is also a principal centre of the British tourist business, receiving perhaps as many visitors as any other in England outside London. So from every point of view, as an historic centre of railways and as a town most notably worth visiting in its own right, York was an admirable place in which to house the new museum – the first national museum to be set up in the English provinces.

The building chosen for it was a former motive-power depot, adjoining the main line from London to Newcastle and Edinburgh (Plate 4). This was made over by British Railways, who skilfully adapted it to its new purpose, at the same time providing additional accommodation. The work moved ahead to a tight schedule. Many exhibits had to be moved by BR from Clapham and from the old museum at York (see Plates 5, 6). The opening was fixed for 27 September 1975, to coincide exactly with the 250th anniversary of the opening of the Stockton & Darlington Railway. With a punctuality in the best tradition of railways, that date was observed, and the ceremony was performed by HRH the Duke of Edinburgh.

The Museum is in Leeman Road, three-quarters of a mile from the centre of the city, ten minutes' walk from the railway station. The building presents a great rectangular mass, which was agreeably cased at the conversion in blue-grey engineering bricks. The entrance is on a level with the road, but above the Main Hall of the Museum, which is approached down a short flight of stairs. At the foot of these is a shop, and beyond that, to the right, the little gallery for temporary exhibitions. The refreshment room adjoins the entrance, to the right of which are the small Front Gallery and the Lecture Room. Above the Main Hall, along the whole of its south side, runs the Long Gallery. Out of doors there are two small display areas, to the left and right of the Main Hall, from which they can be seen through glass. On the other side of Leeman Road is the Peter Allen building (named after the first Chairman of the Museum's Committee), acquired in 1976 as an extension to the Museum, used as a store and still in course of development.

The plan adopted in this book is to describe each of these divisions of the Museum in turn – Main Hall, Long Gallery, Front Gallery, Outdoor Exhibits – concluding with something about the Museum's services, the unending activity that goes on behind the scenes.

There are numerous objects in the Museum that remain static and are likely to continue so for as many years ahead as one can see – two stationary engines, for example; but the collection as a whole is by no means rigidly fixed. One of the merits of its present accommodation, compared with that in the old Museum at York or with the one at Clapham, is that even the very large machines can be readily moved around, or in and out of the Museum itself. So their positions change, and in some cases they go away, perhaps to pay visits to other museums. A few of the locomotives are capable of being put into steam, and they have occasionally gone as far afield as Carnforth, Carlisle, or even further. In the same way, small exhibits sometimes leave the Museum, to be shown elsewhere. New things too are brought in as additions to the permanent display or to replace others that have gone.

It is a problem for most museum curators to decide whether they should keep their exhibitions unchanged, at any rate for long periods of time, so allowing visitors to return again and again, bringing friends with them, certain that they will be able to see what interested them before; or whether to aim deliberately at flexibility and change. There is a good deal to be said on both sides of this question. But the National Railway Museum is a special one: concerned with transport, which always has to do with motion, and conscious that it exists not only to provide a display for visitors but also to act as one of the principal centres of the railway preservation movement, a friend and adviser to the very large numbers of societies and individuals up and down the country who are interested in that activity, which has grown so remarkably in the course of the past thirty years. That help may sometimes take the form of lending a locomotive or some other exhibit; and the Museum is itself a borrower, bringing in, on long or short loan, exhibits that may help to fill a gap in its presentation or to acquire a particular significance at some point of time. A little will be said later of these "external" aspects of the work of the Museum. They are not obvious to visitors, yet they are most important.

2
The Main Hall

I LOCOMOTIVES

The general arrangement of the Main Hall is simple. Anybody who wishes to take it in at once should go up to the Long Gallery on arriving and look down. The whole Hall is then within his view. The two turntables, which were in the building before its conversion, determine the plan: for the machines and vehicles are placed on the tracks leading to them. There are twenty-four tracks converging on the left-hand turntable, close to the entrance; they accommodate locomotives (Plate 8). The other has twenty tracks and is used chiefly for carriages and wagons. Round the walls runs a series of cases, holding models of locomotives and vehicles, an assortment of miscellaneous exhibits, and two stationary engines. The majority of visitors will be drawn first to the locomotives, the most spectacular objects in the Museum. So let us begin with them.

Immediately by the entrance a big locomotive is to be seen that has been sectioned on one side, to display something of the way in which it worked. The machine is one of the Pacific (4-6-2)[1] locomotives of the Southern Railway, of the 'Merchant Navy' class, *Ellerman Lines*, British Railways No. 35029. It is not in its original condition, as designed by O.V.S.Bulleid, but as rebuilt by BR in 1959. Its air-smoothed casing has been removed, and most of Bulleid's special devices – in the valve-gear and its lubrication for example – replaced by others, more conventional (Plate 9).

That is a demonstration of the steam locomotive in one of the ultimate forms it reached in Britain. *Ellerman Lines* had a short life: built in 1949, rebuilt ten years later, withdrawn from service in 1966. Close by it stands one of its earliest ancestors: *Agenoria*,[2] built by Foster Rastrick & Co at Stourbridge in 1829 and readily distinguishable from its fantastically high chimney, far taller than any other in the Museum.

---

1 This is the usual British notation, giving first the number of leading wheels, then of driving and of trailing wheels, always in that order.

2 Its name represents the Greek word for 'courage'.

This is a primitive locomotive; still in an experimental stage yet so soundly designed that it remained in service for over fifty years –even if it was not very exacting service, at the Shutt End Colliery in South Staffordshire. *Agenoria* may claim to have been a pioneer in one respect: its axle-boxes were fitted with what were probably the first mechanical lubricators applied to a locomotive. And it makes an interesting reference to America: for three engines like it were supplied at the same time to the Delaware & Hudson Railroad, and one of them, *Stourbridge Lion*, was the first of any kind to run in the United States. One detail of the finish of *Agenoria* is worth noting: the makers' plate, on the balance-weight of one of the wheels, beautifully decorated and lettered in a late Georgian tradition.

Here then by the entrance these two machines indicate the wide range of interest that the Museum has to offer. A walk round the turntable affords a general view of the locomotives as a whole (not omitting an inspection of one of them from underneath, in the deepened pit). They are not displayed in any special order, of date or type or company. Some will, as it were, have their backs turned; others will be seen chimney first. They seem a very mixed assortment. But none of these locomotives has found its way here by accident. Each is in the Museum for some good reason; it has to justify its inclusion, the precious space it occupies. At the present moment the National Railway Collection comprises about ninety locomotives, and the number is growing (pp. 55–66). The Museum would be entitled to put all these on show at York. But it has not room to do so. Not more than twenty-five are normally accommodated here at any one time. The remainder must either be lent to other museums or preservation societies or kept in store. Naturally the Museum reserves for its own visitors those it considers likely to make the richest and most representative display. So that the locomotives that stand here have won their places in a stiff competition.

Perhaps they are best considered not in order of age or mechanical type but according to the kind of work they were designed to perform. Express passenger engines form the largest single group. They are the most famous, and usually the most striking to look at. Let us begin with them.

They are not among the oldest machines. The express passenger train itself did not emerge until 1845, on the Great Western and Bristol & Exeter Railways, and nothing of that enterprise is to be seen here, unless one reckons in the amazing pair of driving wheels of a later Bristol & Exeter engine mounted outside, close to the entrance: 8 ft 10 in in diameter, they are among the largest wheels ever to be placed under a locomotive and certainly the largest surviving anywhere. The earliest express engine here is No. 1 of the Great Northern Railway, designed by Patrick Stirling and built in 1870. Its single pair of driving wheels is not much smaller (8 ft in diameter). It was unusual among British locomotives, at the time when it was built, in having its cylinders outside and its front end supported on a four-wheeled bogie truck. Both these devices were contrary to Stirling's own normal practice. But he had good reasons for what he did here, reasons arising from the distribution of the machine's weight on the track and the limitations of the narrow British loading gauge. They are all well analysed in the description placed beside the locomotive (Plate 19).

A more orthodox express locomotive of the Mid-Victorian age comes from the North Eastern Railway: 2-4-0 No. 910 of 1872. This machine takes us down a long corridor in history. Not long after it was built, it participated in the celebrations of the Jubilee of the Stockton & Darlington Railway in 1875. It was withdrawn from service in 1925, appearing at Darlington in the procession of locomotives commemorating the Stockton & Darlington's centenary in July of that year. In 1975 it contributed to the 150th anniversary of the same event at Shildon: not this time under its own steam. That is not all. The designer of No. 910 was Edward Fletcher. In the Front Gallery of the Museum hangs his portrait in old age – blunt and four-square; and beside it the original indenture of his apprenticeship to George Stephenson in 1825. So here in this one machine we have, concentrated as one might say, 150 years of history.

Back again to the unorthodox: to the Brighton Company's *Gladstone* of 1882, the only express engine here (and one of the very few ever to run in Britain) in which the coupled wheels were placed in front (Plate 10). The designer, William Stroudley, argued that it had enabled him to achieve a better distribution of weight since locomotives were heavier at the front end and the big wheels could give greater support and stability. *Gladstone* and the thirty-five other engines of the class rendered steady and meritorious service for a long time on the Company's main lines. When they were new they hauled the 8.45 am express up from Brighton to London Bridge, probably then the heaviest train in daily service in the country. As late as the 1920s they were occasionally still being used on the boat trains to and from Newhaven. Notice the name of the driver, William Love, painted inside the cab. It was the Company's practice to assign each locomotive to one driver, who regarded it as in a sense his

own and consequently took an intense pride in its upkeep and performance: one indication of the personal nature of the railway service,
which helped to give it the peculiar character it bore.

Already, when *Gladstone* was built, things were beginning to change.
Stroudley designed well for the needs of his own railway; but if the
8.45 from Brighton was a heavy train it was not a fast one. By the 1880s
it was coming to be accepted that in Britain an 'express train' was one
that ran at a minimum speed of 40mph, including stops; this Brighton
express only just managed to qualify for the title, travelling non-stop.
Elsewhere, north of the Thames, trains were running much faster and
also growing heavier. Small engines were still often employed on them,
and continued to be down to the end of the century: like the London &
North Western Company's *Hardwicke* (now in the Museum), which
put up dazzling performances in the Race to Scotland in 1895. But
those feats were in exceptional service, with the lightest possible trains.
In ordinary conditions much more powerful locomotives were coming
to be demanded. Two of them are in the Museum, both put into service
in 1893: one on the North Eastern Railway, the other on the London
& South Western.

The North Eastern locomotive (No.1621) was the heaviest express
engine yet seen in Britain, with ample adhesion and plenty of power from
the steam raised in a large boiler. Engines of this type also showed
splendidly in the Race of 1895, between York and Edinburgh. Two
brothers, T.W. and Wilson Worsdell, served the North Eastern Company in succession as Locomotive Engineers; this machine was designed
by the younger of them. One of the outstanding things they did (under
American influence) was to improve the provision for the locomotive
crews on the footplate. One has only to compare the little cab of
Fletcher's No.910 with the one on this engine to see what this meant.
The enginemen are now completely protected overhead, and the side-
sheets have been extended, with big windows to the cab. The driving
of steam locomotives was always apt to be a test of endurance: cold and
hot work by turns, rough when the engine rode badly, and for the fire-
man an exhausting grind of labour, almost uninterrupted. The Worsdells
were leaders in a long-overdue effort to ease the task.

The London & South Western machine, No.563, was built in 1893
and designed by William Adams, one of the best locomotive engineers
of his time, particularly for the express trains over the steeply-graded
line from Salisbury to Exeter. Equipped with his well-designed bogie,
it ran steadily and smoothly–though high-speed exploits were seldom

called for by the South Western Company comparable with those on the lines to Scotland. Adams's 'Vortex' blast-pipe was another of the good features of this engine: an effective device for spreading the draught evenly. These machines were powerful and robust. They stood up to their work well, and this one was not taken out of service until 1945.

In the 1890s the British railways were beginning to face serious economic difficulties. Their expenditure was rising rapidly, from new safety precautions and higher labour costs as well as from faster services, and their revenue was not keeping pace with it. They were willing to look closely at any device that seemed to promise economy. One was compounding: the designing of a locomotive in such a way as to allow it to use its steam twice over, at high and at low pressure. The London & North Western Company went furthest in adopting the practice, at the instance of F.W.Webb, its Chief Mechanical Engineer. But the results there were not satisfactory. Only one British company made a success of compounding, and then with a single type of locomotive. That was the Midland, and the first of its compound engines, No.1000, is here–not as it was originally built, however, in 1902, but in a later form, somewhat modified. It is a 4-4-0 with three cylinders, the high-pressure one inside and the two larger low-pressure ones outside.

At the same time fresh efforts were being made to increase the steaming power of the locomotive by the provision of larger boilers and bigger fire-grates–a task more difficult than might appear because of the restricted British loading gauge. The Great Northern 4-4-2 (Atlantic) type locomotive No.251 (1902) exemplifies both these developments and in its present form a third too: the superheater, which came into widespread use in Britain from about 1910 onwards, for raising the heat of the steam on its way from the boiler to the cylinders.

At this point the initiative in British express locomotive development passed clearly, for the time being, to the Great Western Railway. That cannot be followed at York, but it is to be seen in the locomotive *Lode Star* at Swindon and in *Caerphilly Castle* at the Science Museum in London. Though *Flying Scotsman* (1923) is an occasional visitor to York, the story of the development of the express passenger engine is not fully resumed there until the 1930s, with the great Pacific (4-6-2) locomotives *Mallard* and *Duchess of Hamilton*, followed by *Ellerman Lines*.

Mallard, No.4468 of the London & North Eastern Railway, is perhaps the most widely celebrated object in the whole Museum: for it holds the world's record for steam traction, of 126mph achieved in 1938, and that is never now likely to be surpassed. It is one of a series of engines designed by (Sir) Nigel Gresley for working the high-speed trains that the Company put on, from 1935 onwards, between London and Newcastle, Edinburgh, and Leeds. These trains set a new standard of excellence. They were streamlined, and strictly limited in weight. The first of them, the 'Silver Jubilee' of 1935, ran from London to Newcastle in four hours, at 67mph. That was a speed quite unprecedented in Britain for any train in regular service over such a long distance. Yet acceleration has gone so much further since then that four hours has become more than the *average* time taken by the quicker trains on that journey today.

The London & North Eastern Company's rival the London Midland & Scottish replied with a corresponding high-speed train between London and Glasgow. That too was streamlined, and worked by Pacific locomotives designed by (Sir) William Stanier. *Duchess of Hamilton* is one of them. If the speed of the LMS train was slightly lower than its competitor's, it was heavier and its route a good deal harder. It called for locomotive work of at least as high an order, and got it. After the war the streamlined casing of these engines was removed, and this one appears in that later condition.

The Stanier Pacifics were the most powerful express engines ever to work in Britain. A careful and judicious comparison between the LMS and LNER Pacifics is given in the Museum's admirable publication *Gresley and Stanier*, by John Bellwood and David Jenkinson. Here we are at the end of the story of the high-speed steam locomotive in Britain. It is a splendid climax.

———

Great Britain is a small island; and the average railway journey has always been short. For this reason the tank engine came to find much favour: carrying its own fuel and water with no need for a tender, and able to be driven in either direction without being turned round. From the 1870s onwards it began to be adopted widely, in London for suburban traffic and in all kinds of short-distance service. The Museum has three examples of tank engines used extensively on passenger trains.

The earliest is the Brighton Company's little six-wheeled engine *Boxhill*, one of a class of fifty nicknamed 'Terriers', designed by William Stroudley and built in 1872–80. Their particular assignment was to lines with very lightly laid track, especially the East London line through the Thames Tunnel and the South London, from Victoria to London Bridge via Brixton. Though very small (their weight was less than 25 tons) they proved entirely adequate to their duties, until loads grew too heavy for them towards the end of the century. Later in life they gravitated to country branch lines, especially again those where axle loads were severely limited, like the Hayling Island branch near Portsmouth. A number of them were sold to other companies. One has found its way to the Canadian Railroad Museum at Montreal.

The Lancashire & Yorkshire 2-4-2 tank engine No. 1008 is a different sort of machine. Its company's system was a particularly dense one, and like the Brighton it adopted the tank engine in the 1870s. This engine, built in 1889, is the prototype of one of the largest classes of passenger tank engine ever developed in Britain. There were 330 of them, the last built in 1911. They were used in all kinds of passenger service, including expresses. But they proved unsteady on curves at high speeds, and they were taken off the fastest trains. For the rest, they gave thoroughly good service all over Lancashire and across the Pennines to Leeds and Bradford for over half a century.

The third of these tank engines, Great Eastern Railway No. 87, is like *Boxhill* a six-wheeled machine, but a good deal more powerful (Plate 13). The Great Eastern Company operated into and out of Liverpool Street station in London one of the densest suburban services to be found anywhere, bringing countless thousands of commuters into the City from Hertfordshire and Essex. The planning of the service was ingenious, its operation disciplined and punctual. It was worked entirely by tank engines, able to take one train into its terminus and another away in the minimum time, without being turned. The earlier engines had four coupled wheels, but in 1889 the Locomotive Engineer, James Holden, tried out a six-coupled engine, originally designed for shunting, in this passenger service. The experiment was successful, and new engines of the type were built to undertake the work. No. 87 is one of the last batch, turned out in 1904. They were able to handle very heavy trains – carrying in the rush hours 800 passengers and more apiece. This machine represents something more than a phase of railway practice, and a technique. It is a memorial of the development of Greater London.

Notable as these three locomotives are, they do not represent at all fully the development of the tank engine in Britain. Not one designed for goods service is here, nor one that could be called large; the latest of them was built in 1904. Other important machines of the kind are to be seen elsewhere. At Caerphilly, for example, there is one of the 0-6-2 tank engines that helped to make South Wales, for a time, the greatest exporter of coal in the world; at Bressingham in Norfolk one of the big 2-6-4 engines built by the London Midland & Scottish Company for work on the line between Fenchurch Street and Southend in the 1930s. But the tank engine was employed above all in shunting, in the vital work of the goods yard, around collieries and in all forms of industry. Its role here was so modest that few people showed much interest in preserving any examples of it in this shape. However, one good shunting engine is to be seen in the Glasgow Museum of Transport, and a number of them are at work on the preserved railways.

On the large British railways in the Victorian age it was usual to build locomotives specifically for passenger or for goods traffic. As the machines grew older they might find themselves switched, on branch lines, to kinds of work for which they had not originally been intended. Towards the end of the nineteenth century, however, the 'mixed traffic' locomotive began to be designed on a large scale. Two good examples of this type of machine are in the Museum at York.

The first comes from the Great Eastern Railway (No.490), and it was designed to deal with all kinds of traffic on the long rural cross-country lines of East Anglia: from Colchester to Cambridge, for example. A hundred of these engines were built in 1891–1902, and they did their work well. Years afterwards under the London & North Eastern administration some found their way to the steeply-graded line from Darlington to Penrith, which ran over the Pennines at Stainmore. There too they gave satisfaction. They never took the limelight, as express engines often did; but they were admirably straightforward machines, and it was wise to preserve one of them.

The other mixed-traffic engine is much more sophisticated: No.4771 *Green Arrow* of the London & North Eastern, built in 1936. The engines of this class were intended for fast goods trains; but having proved themselves there satisfactorily, they came to be used in express service too and they continued to undertake both kinds of work efficiently until the days of the steam engine drew to an end.

The oldest freight locomotive to be seen at York is Furness Railway No.3, nicknamed *Coppernob* for a reason that will be obvious to anyone who looks at it. This is the only example to be seen in Great Britain (there is also one in Ireland) of Edward Bury's distinctive type. Bury's firm in Liverpool specialised in machines of this sort: small and cheap in prime cost, though strongly built, and mounted on frames made of bars of iron, not of plates. The bar-frame did not ultimately prevail in Britain, but it became standard in North America. *Coppernob* was built in 1846 and employed in its early days on passenger as well as goods trains. It remained in service until 1898, when it was probably the oldest locomotive still running regularly anywhere in Britain. It was preserved on withdrawal, mounted at Barrow-in-Furness station, damaged there in an air-raid, and now rests where it ought to be, in a national museum (Plate 12).

Not long after *Coppernob* was built a new pattern of freight locomotive emerged: still with the cylinders inside the frames, but with six coupled wheels, the last pair placed behind the firebox. This 0-6-0 type came to be the standard one used, with many variations in size and power, on every large English railway, and extensively in Scotland too. (South Wales had a special freight engine of its own: see pp. 13–14.) The first of these machines were built in 1848; the last exactly 100 years later. Here they are represented by one of class P3 of the North Eastern Railway, to be seen as a model in Case 17 (Plate 15).

The only Great Western locomotive at York (the main collection being at Swindon) is a freight engine of a bigger type: 2-8-0 No.2818. This is one of a type first produced in 1903 to the design of G. J. Churchward. It continued to be found satisfactory, almost unchanged except for the addition of a superheater, for the rest of the Company's existence. The last of these machines were built in 1942. All through that time, and for twenty years more, they slogged along, down and up through the Severn Tunnel, on the heavy coal trains from South Wales.

The 2-10-0 built by the nationalised railways represents the ultimate development of the British freight engine. It was the last of the twelve standard designs laid down by British Railways, and by general consent the most successful: not only a good weight-hauler, but capable on occasion of a high turn of speed. If more time had been available, to experiment and improve not only details of design but also the handling of the engines by their crews, it might well have come to be reckoned one of the classic types in British railway history. But time was not given. The first of the class appeared in 1954; 250 more were built, but they had all been withdrawn from service by 1968, displaced by diesel-powered locomotives. No. 92220, included in the National Collection

was the last steam locomotive to be built for British Railways, turned
out of Swindon Works in 1960 and given the appropriate name (borne
also by one of the earliest engines on the Great Western Railway)
Evening Star. It is sad to think that the working life of this impressive
machine (it cost £30,000 to build) was just five years.

That is the end of the history of steam locomotives in Britain. The first
impression the display of them will make on many visitors to York must
be of their variety, in size and shape and colour. They are indeed painted
in shades of almost every colour one could think of: blue, brown, red,
black, many greens. (Even white was used once, for a short time, on
Webb's compound *Queen Empress* in 1897. Canary yellow, picked out
with purple and gold, appeared in 1910 on the Shanghai–Nanking
Railway.) These colours are the symbols of competitive private companies. Each of the major companies sought to differentiate its machines
in this way.

It was only in the opening years of the twentieth century that publicity came to be recognised as important to a railway. The styles of
painting and decoration of the older locomotives had been evolved long
before that time, and not, at the beginning, for purposes of advertisement. The ironwork had to be painted, the brass and copper polished,
or it would rust and corrode. Two colours had long been favoured for
such purposes on machinery: black or green. Those two always remained
the most popular for locomotives. They were adopted by two-thirds of
the leading companies in Great Britain.

But the blacks and greens differed. Some blacks were lined out in
other colours as well–red, white, and grey. The greens to be seen here
range widely from the lightest shades, on the North Eastern and the
South Western, to the rich dark colour adopted by the Great Western,
and on British Railways' *Evening Star*. The Southern, under Bulleid,
evolved a sickly malachite, displayed on a model in Case 95.

Of the other colours the Midland's crimson lake became one of the
most famous. It emerged in 1881–83 in place of a dark green, and it was
adopted as a means of economy: it halved painting costs. It can be seen
here on the 4-4-0 compound No. 1000* and on the two Midland carriages.
Some of the liveries involved extremely elaborate combinations of

---

* Locomotives and vehicles marked with an asterisk may be away from York
for some time after the publication of this book.

colours. The Brighton Company's engines here exemplify that. Eight are used altogether. But the most complicated of them all is on the South Eastern & Chatham locomotive No. 737 (Plate 11). Eleven separate tints can be counted here, excluding further shades on the coat of arms, and not to mention the copper and brass work. This was one of the first express engines designed for the South Eastern & Chatham Managing Committee – a combination of two dirty and unloved railways, which was anxious to live down their past. The machine was an impressive advertisement of new intentions; a piece of publicity indeed.

All these matters of style and decoration are, of course, to be judged personally. Let me say what I think myself. To my mind the livery of No.737 is a trifle too elaborate, one or two of these eleven colours – certainly the milk-chocolate shade on the frame – unpleasing. I regret that this particular locomotive should be thus tricked out, like a fine woman slightly over-dressed: since for me it is, in line and proportion, the most beautiful machine in the whole Museum. Every part of it is precisely right in relation to all the rest. Its flowing curves set off the clean straight lines; the boiler mountings – chimney, dome, safety valve – are right in size, in their placing and their relationship to one another; the tender matches the engine exactly. Seen in a black-and-white photograph, the locomotive is a masterpiece, the British late-Victorian express engine at the classic point of its perfection.

Near by, however, there are two locomotives that wear a much simpler livery, which seems to me in its kind perfect: the pair from the Great Eastern Railway. Here the colours are four: black, gold, scarlet, and the prevailing royal blue. The more one looks at them the more delightful that combination of colours becomes. It is applied with the utmost restraint – avoiding the use of white, which looks good on black but is too assertive on almost any other colour. The bright scarlet is used only a little, but to precisely-judged effect. The whole makes a complete harmony: something that can fairly be called a work of art.

These are personal opinions. Perhaps few people will agree with them. No matter. Make up your own mind.

––––––

So far all the machines discussed here have been steam locomotives. But other forms of propulsion are also represented at York: electric, diesel, and gas-turbine.

The electric locomotive here may claim to be the oldest, designed specifically for freight traffic, that survives anywhere (Plate 17). It is one of a pair built for the North Eastern Railway to work the Quayside Branch at Newcastle; a specially awkward line, for it was steep, sharply-graded, and largely in tunnel, which made it almost intolerable to the drivers of steam locomotives. The two electric engines were built in 1904, to the design of (Sir) Vincent Raven, advised by Charles Merz. They never worked anywhere except on this one short line, with a normal stint of some sixteen hours a day, twelve of them spent in shunting. They did their job admirably for sixty years, when they gave place to diesel engines. This machine has four 160 hp motors, and it took current at 600 volts DC. With its bow collector and wooden cab, it may look archaic now; but it was important when it was new. Its introduction followed immediately on the conversion of the chief Newcastle suburban passenger services to electric traction. The North Eastern Company then began to contemplate the use of that power much more widely. It equipped the line from Shildon to Middlesbrough for the electric haulage of freight traffic, a task completed by 1915, and worked out a bigger plan of electrifying the whole line from Newcastle to York. A model of the experimental express locomotive Raven built for this purpose is to be seen in the Long Gallery (Case 115). The idea, however, was abandoned after the first World War.

The London & North Eastern Company (into which the North Eastern was merged in 1923) undertook a considerable piece of electrification of the same sort on the line from Manchester to Sheffield through the Woodhead Tunnel. Work was started before the second war broke out, and then suspended. The task was resumed when peace came, and electric trains began to run through the Pennines in 1954. The system adopted was direct current at 1500 volts, with overhead transmission. A class of fifty-seven locomotives was built for freight work on the line; one of these machines, No.26020,* has been brought here to York.

Britain was not quick to adopt the diesel locomotive. It was tried experimentally in various forms during the 1930s, but it did not pass into general use until after nationalisation. Its merits in shunting work were apparent, and a very large number of diesel-engined machines for this type of service have now been built. One of them has found its way into the Museum: diesel-mechanical No.03090. which came out of Doncaster works in 1960 and was withdrawn in 1976 (Plate 16). Its short life does not indicate that it was unsuccessful; it was due to the shrinkage of the system, which reduced the demand for machines of its type. It continues to render useful service inside the Museum in moving large exhibits.

This small machine has now been joined by others, much bigger: among them one of the "Western" diesel-hydraulic locomotives,* introduced in 1961. The Regions of the nationalised system were left some freedom to devise their own policies on motive power, and the Western Region adopted diesel-hydraulic transmission for its passenger locomotives, whilst diesel-electric was used everywhere else. This class was the last and most powerful of those built for the Region. The British Railways Board presently decided to use a smaller number of types of standard locomotives all over the system. These machines were then displaced, well before the end of their natural life, by diesel-electric locomotives of classes 47 and 50.

We have moved here into very recent times. The Museum displays the working of railways not only in the past but also in the present, even looking forward into the future. We have become accustomed in the last few years to the Inter-City 125 trains (running past the Museum for three years now). They were developed side by side with another high-speed unit, the Advanced Passenger Train (APT), which was more revolutionary. Its suspension includes a tilting device, allowing it to take curves half as fast again as a normal train; and its hydro-kinetic brakes can bring it to a stop in the ordinary distance from speeds in the region of 150mph. An experimental unit (powered by gas turbines) went through exhaustive tests. When those were completed in 1976, work began on the building of three sets, electrically powered, to run between London and Glasgow. The life of this unit was then over, and it passed into the keeping of the Museum. Rightly: for it is already an important monument in the history of technology.

II ROLLING STOCK, MODELS, AND OTHER EXHIBITS

To walk from the APT to the early passenger vehicles is to make a very long journey backwards in time and spirit. There are replicas here of two belonging to the Liverpool & Manchester Railway, built for the celebration of its centenary in 1930: one first-class, one second. The first-class vehicle is in many ways a new version of a horse-drawn coach. Its three compartments are modelled on a coach interior and the styling of the body outside with its curving panels is exactly the same as appeared on all such vehicles, public or private. The Company engaged a coachbuilder, Nathaniel Worsdell (whose sons we have encountered as

Locomotive Engineers on the North Eastern Railway), to direct this part of its business. It was clearly intended to make the railway carriages look as much like the horse-drawn coaches as possible; passengers by the new means of transport could thus feel at home in them. But there were important differences, concealed behind the apparent similarities. Each unit was composed, in effect, of the bodies of *three* horse coaches, though with no provision for carrying 'outside' passengers on the roof. That practice was not unknown on some early railways; but it was clearly undesirable owing to the dangers from the locomotives' cinders, and from low bridges, and it did not continue long. The accommodation in each compartment was larger and more comfortable than that afforded by the road vehicles. Six passengers were provided for, each in an arm-chair, compared with four, at closer quarters and without arm-rests, earlier. But the biggest difference lay in the frame, which was constructed of iron and wood; it had to be made very strong, to withstand the pull of the locomotive, the jolting when the train stopped, and the wear-and-tear of shunting. So the early railway carriage was by no means a horse-drawn coach simply transferred to rails; it was from the outset something different.

The second-class vehicle, painted sky-blue, is a mere wooden box on an iron frame, open to the four winds. It is not provided with seats. Within a few years such accommodation, even for passengers travelling at the lowest rates, became obsolete, and they were at least closed in and given wooden benches to sit on.

The Liverpool & Manchester Company maintained two classes of travel only. Many of its successors offered three–a few four. The class distinctions appear very plainly in the Museum from its set of vehicles of the Bodmin & Wadebridge Railway, which may perhaps be dated about 1840. The accommodation they offer is extremely cramped; but the railway was a very short one, only seven miles long. The buffers on these vehicles are 'dumb', i.e. unsprung, though on more sophisticated railways like the Liverpool & Manchester the spring buffer had already arrived, making an important contribution to the ease and comfort of passenger travel.

The greatest luxury attainable in early days is shown in the vehicle built by the London & Birmingham Railway for the use of Queen Adelaide in 1842. The Company went to Hooper's, one of the most famous London coachbuilders of the time, for the bodywork, and the finish of it was superb: the handles were gold-plated, and the armorial bearings painted by hand. The vehicle is in three sections: a coupé at one end, a four-seater in the middle, and the Queen's own compartment at the other. This affords a primitive bed, convertible from sitting accommodation, the feet projecting into a boot. Such 'bed carriages' were used on a number of railways for less august passengers, until they were superseded by sleeping cars from the 1870s onwards.

The ordinary carriage of the 1840s is well represented by one from the Stockton & Darlington Railway: a composite with a first-class compartment in the centre, flanked by two second-class. It cost £230 to build, or about £8 for each place it afforded. It must have earned that capital many times over in the course of its life (Plate 21).

In most of these vehicles there is provision for a guard to sit aloft, where he could survey the train, keep an eye on the luggage piled on the roof (it was apt to catch fire from the engine's sparks), and apply the brake to his carriage. It was a nastily exposed position, and presently the guard and the luggage were removed to the inside of the train.

An oddity of the 1860s is to be seen here: the 'dandy car' hauled by horses on the Port Carlisle branch until–the date is extraordinary–1914. Here the third-class passengers were once more put outside, but since there was no engine there were no smuts, and the journey lasted only twenty minutes, so the discomfort was bearable.

The railway carriage did not fully emancipate itself from the horse-drawn coach until the Mid-Victorian age. The North London Railway directors' saloon of 1872 is the earliest example at York of what may be called an entirely railway vehicle, its independence of character made more emphatic by the choice of teak for its construction, a hardwood unknown to any coach-builder and one that came to be widely favoured because its natural oils enabled it to resist the weather and so obviated painting.

That is a special vehicle, for the use of top management. The carriages offered to the ordinary North London traveller were Spartan in their hardness, though like this one extremely well built. An example of good accommodation provided for long-distance passengers in the 1880s is given in the six-wheeled Midland carriage, glowing in its crimson lake. The Midland Company had done much to cheapen and popularise travel in the seventies, abolishing second class and upgrading third by making it more comfortable. This vehicle is a composite, for first- and third-class passengers, with a luggage compartment in the middle. It is still lighted by oil lamps, though carriages of this kind were fitted to burn gas from 1892 onwards. We have not yet arrived here at the luxuries of steam heating, the lavatory, and the corridor; but the accommodation afforded by a vehicle like this was a long way removed from the bare wooden box still provided for the third-class passenger, even over long distances, in the sixties. It is all of a piece with the political and social changes of the time. Though the railway maintained class distinctions, it was in a deep sense a democratising force (Plate 23).

There are two other mid-Victorian vehicles here, both used in passenger train service yet neither of them designed to carry passengers. One is a Great Northern brake van, six-wheeled like the Midland carriage, and like it admirably restored, in this case in the railway workshops at York. The other vehicle is of exceptional interest. It is a Travelling Post Office,* built for the West Coast Postal train, which went into service between London and Aberdeen on 1 July 1885. This was the longest regular run ever made by a pure mail train (it carried no passengers at all south of Holytown in Scotland). The Travelling Post Office, which allowed mails to be picked up, sorted, and put out *en route* without stopping, was first tried out on the Grand Junction Railway in 1839. Here the device is seen in its perfected form: with gangways for access to adjacent vehicles (turning the whole train, in effect, into a single long sorting office), the equipment at the side for putting out mail-bags, the net for taking them in. This was one of the railways' important contributions to the growth and improvement of the postal service – with all that that came to mean, in terms of communication and knowledge, of political and economic power, in the Victorian age.

The vehicle is interesting also for a technical reason. It is mounted on eight wheels, four at each end; but the two pairs do not form bogies. F. W. Webb of the London & North Western Railway, which built the carriage, entirely disapproved of them. Instead, the outer pairs of wheels were given his 'radial axle-boxes', which allowed them some side-play, whilst keeping the inner pair rigid. His contention was that this made the vehicle ride better and more safely, but his example was little followed on other railways (Plate 24).

Another important carriage, for the railway service alone, stands near by: the dynamometer car used for testing locomotives, built by the North Eastern Company in 1906. This is a truly historic vehicle, for it was used in all the successive trials leading to the introduction of the high-speed service of 1935 (see p. 12) and ran behind *Mallard* when the world's speed record was set up in 1938. A particularly full and informative account of the vehicle is placed behind it, describing also the elaborate instruments it contains (Plate 22).

Two more vehicles designed for ordinary passengers, though reaching an exceptionally high standard of coach-building, are also exhibited here. Both went into service in 1914. One of them is a restaurant car–or to use the term emblazoned on its sides, a 'dining carriage'–for the Midland Railway. It is mounted on a pair of six-wheeled bogies, and its roof is of the 'clerestorey' type, to which the Midland adhered after it had ceased to be fashionable elsewhere. The craftsmanship of the bodywork and its fittings is excellent. It stands foursquare in the tradition that reaches back to the coach-building of the eighteenth century. The same is true of much of the decoration and equipment that has survived inside; and anyone interested in the evolution of domestic appliances will appreciate the selection of them to be seen in its kitchen.

The Midland Company introduced the Pullman car into England from America in the 1870s. It did not maintain the connection very long, ending its contract with G.M.Pullman and buying up his cars in 1888. Other companies acted differently, however. One was the South Eastern & Chatham, and here is a Pullman car, *Topaz*, built by the Birmingham Railway Carriage & Wagon Company for service on the line from London to Folkestone and Dover (Plate 28). It is constructed differently from any other passenger vehicle in the Museum, following the American practice of making the body and underframe one, whereas in Britain it was usual to keep the two separate. *Topaz* was also in a certain sense old-fashioned in that its body was built wholly of timber, at a time when steel had come to enter largely into the construction of carriages for express service in Britain. The car (Pullmans always retained, even in this country, their American appellation of 'cars'–they were never 'coaches' or 'carriages') accommodated twenty-four first-class passengers. Those who remember travelling in vehicles of this kind, in the boat trains, or to Sheffield or Cardiff or Bournemouth, will always think of them as providing a quite exceptional degree of comfort, and remember too the gentle creaking of their timber as they moved.

One other group of passenger vehicles remains: the large royal saloons. They differ from the rest because they were intended only for occasional use, by the royal family; hence they were of course constructed to the highest standards of craftsmanship and comfort. Provision of this kind was made for the ruler of every country in the nineteenth century–not in monarchies alone: there were Presidential cars in the United States. But political changes have destroyed and dispersed them. A few others are preserved elsewhere: a narrow-gauge one at Hamar in Norway, for example, several in Germany and Sweden, Pope Pius IX's saloon in the Municipal Museum of Rome.

Most of these vehicles are small four-wheelers, very different from the huge and highly sophisticated carriages we are now going to examine. There are three of these, and two others, though not strictly royal saloons, should be considered with them.

They were all built by one company, the London & North Western, in its works at Wolverton–though before 1914 most large companies on whose lines the sovereign travelled at all frequently also had their own royal saloons. If one series only could be kept, this is undoubtedly the best. These were the vehicles most often used by Queen Victoria and her successors in their long night journeys, made several times a year, from Windsor to Balmoral in Scotland; journeys that have been described in minute detail, once and for all, by G.P.Neele, a London & North Western official who had a large share in organising them from 1863 to 1895, in his *Railway Reminiscences*. Anyone who has read those descriptions will turn with fascinated pleasure to the oldest of this group of saloons, the one used by Queen Victoria from 1869 to her death.

It went through one important change, and one only, in her life-time. Originally there were two vehicles, each mounted on six wheels, connected by an enclosed gangway–the first of that kind seen in Britain. Then in 1895 the two bodies were amalgamated into one, and the whole mounted on a pair of six-wheeled bogies: the form in which we see it now. The Queen's tenacious conservatism forbade any further changes, and the whole remains exactly as she knew it. The interior furnishing is very notable, especially the drawing-room in the centre, with the prevailing tone given by the richest blue watered silk. Unfortunately it must not be kept highly illuminated, since the fabric is fragile and easily damaged by light. This is not only a sumptuous royal railway carriage; it may claim to be one of the most perfect mid-Victorian interiors to be found, in a house or anywhere else in Britain (Plate 30).

When the Queen died, there was a change. In its style and appointments this is very much a woman's vehicle, and her son Edward VII preferred something different. The London & North Western then built a new pair of saloons for him and Queen Alexandra, and they were brought into use in 1903. Some account seems to have been taken, in designing them, of a special vehicle the Company had built three years earlier for the use of the Duke of Sutherland, one of its directors, who travelled a great deal between his properties in northern Scotland, Trentham in Staffordshire, and London. This is also in the National Collection and is sometimes to be seen at York. It must however be noted that the royal saloons of 1903 have not retained their original decoration. They were redecorated to a new scheme in the 1930s, under the eye of Queen Mary. Beside them stands another twelve-wheeled saloon. This was constructed as an ordinary dining car by the London & North Western Company in 1900, shown at the Paris Exhibition of that year, and then presently allocated to the royal train.

These magnificent vehicles exemplify the highest attainable standards of coach-building at the time–almost, one might say, with no expense spared. Taken in conjunction with the big models adjoining (also built at Wolverton), with *Topaz* and the Midland dining car, they form a demonstration of the conditions of railway travel at their most luxurious at the end of the railway's golden age, which was terminated by the first World War.

The Main Hall has two more large exhibits to show–stationary engines, mounted on the walls–and a considerable number of smaller ones. In early days the stationary engine was the rival of the locomotive in railway operation. That was the point of the Rainhill trials of 1829, to see which could work trains better. The matter was settled then clearly in favour of the locomotive, *Rocket*; but there were nevertheless some conditions in which the stationary engine was more successful, and it continued in use here and there for another century and more. It was well suited for haulage on very steep inclines. The two machines displayed here were both used for that purpose. The one close to the entrance worked the Weatherhill incline, which was as steep as 1 in 13, and was brought into use in 1834. The Stanhope & Tyne Railway, which installed it, was an extremely curious one. On the thirty-eight miles of its line from Weardale down to the coast at South Shields it employed all the varieties of haulage then known–horse, gravity-working, stationary engine, locomotive. It was neither a well-planned nor a well-managed concern, and it went bankrupt, nearly ruining the great engineer Robert Stephenson, who was one of its original shareholders. The railway was closed entirely in 1841–45. It was then somewhat improved, modernised, and extended. This winding-engine continued in service for over eighty years.

The other stationary steam engine here was designed by Robert Stephenson for use at the western end of the Leicester & Swannington Railway, built in 1833 and maintained until 1947. It is of a quite different type. The cylinder of the Weatherhill engine is placed vertically, which was the usual plan; here it is horizontal. These two machines afford a good view of the way in which engineers produced their own solutions to the problems that faced them. Both have been meticulously restored by Messrs Riley & Son, millwrights of Heywood in Lancashire, for exhibition here, and they are in working order, though with electric, not steam power.

A series of cases extends round the outer walls of the Main Hall, containing models and photographs of locomotives and rolling-stock: a useful complement to the full-sized exhibits placed in front of them. First, immediately by the entrance, come demonstrations of some of the essential parts of a locomotive's equipment: valves and valve-gear, the boiler and the methods of raising steam and controlling it, lubricators, continuous brakes. Here is an admirable exposition, pithy, clear, and precisely informative on the basic technology of the locomotive.

Then begins a series of models. One, of the Grand Junction engine *Wildfire*, is among the earliest models of a locomotive in existence anywhere, made in Birmingham in 1839. It is a working model, designed to run by steam; not accurate in every detail, yet very far from crude (Plate 14). A group of machines built in the 1860s is especially welcome here since the Museum has no full-size engines of those years to show; two 4-4-0 tank engines from London (both of exceptionally fine quality as models), and a 2-4-0 passenger engine from the Manchester Sheffield & Lincolnshire Railway. Models can be admirably used to fill in the gaps in the Museum's display. Here is one instance. Another is to be seen close by: the London & North Western compound locomotive *Jubilee*. Most of F.W.Webb's compounds were withdrawn rapidly after his retirement in 1902, or converted into simple engines. His successor, George Whale, was chiefly anxious to get rid of them, on account of the difficulties they gave in service, and the notion of preserving one would have seemed to him laughable. So the compounds all went to the scrap heap. Whale's excellent simple engines went the same way, in their turn. All this was a pity. But here at least we have models of the two types: *Jubilee*, much the more powerful on paper though with a boiler not large enough to provide steam for its four cylinders; *Precursor*, Whale's engine, rightly proportioned in all its parts, robust and free from complexities. The last engine of its type, *Sirocco*, was broken up only in 1949. Had it survived a year or two longer it might well have been saved by preservationists.

A word may perhaps be interjected here about the quality of the presentation in these wall-cases. It has all been elegantly designed, and the information is conveyed with thoughtful care, partly by means of the general back panels (which also include some good pictures of trains in service) and partly by detailed labels. Everything has been well considered, and the technical descriptions, both here and on the large stands that are placed beside most of the locomotives and vehicles, are outstandingly good. Without them, the small exhibits would appear to be no more than a random sample of miscellaneous objects; with them, the series takes on coherence and meaning.

The series continues with two models of British Atlantic locomotives: Aspinall's, with inside cylinders, for the Lancashire & Yorkshire Railway and Wilson Worsdell's V class for the North Eastern. The four amalgamated companies of the inter-war years are represented by *Flying Scotsman*, *Royal Scot*, *King George V*, and *Lancing* (one of the admirable 'Schools' class of the Southern Railway), together with a freight engine of unusual interest: a Beyer-Garratt, a double locomotive (2-6-0—0-6-2), built for the London Midland & Scottish Company. It was one of a class of thirty-three, designed to haul the very heavy coal trains up from Toton in Nottinghamshire to London. A model of another Garratt locomotive from the South African Railways, to be compared with this one, is in the Long Gallery, Case 107. The varied types of such articulated locomotives are excellently described on a panel at the back of the case here. The long series comes to an end with a 2-6-4 tank engine, built for British Railways to what was in most respects a design of the LMS (a two-cylinder version of the machine referred to on p. 14); and with *Britannia*, one of the nationalised railways' standard Pacifics.

Among the models of carriages, one is outstanding in quality and historic interest: that of the North Union Railway's first-class carriage, made in the Company's workshops at Preston in 1842. Its detailing and finish are superb: in the upholstery of the seats, for example. And the arrangement of the buffers is interesting, the whole beam and not the individual buffers being sprung. Beside it is a London & Birmingham vehicle, again a first-class one of three compartments, but of larger proportions – disguised however because the model is made to a smaller scale. The story is then continued with some vehicles for less wealthy passengers: the wooden model of a Great Eastern four-wheeler (such as was hauled by the tank engine No. 87, close by; see Plate 25) and the coach also used in the suburban service of the London Chatham & Dover Railway. Then come the main-line bogie vehicles, first of the years before 1914 and then of the large companies after 1923. The steel chassis of a North Eastern carriage shows the elaborate construction clearly. The London Midland & Scottish and London & North Eastern Companies are represented by sleeping cars; the Great Western by one of the 'Sunshine' vehicles built for the Cornish Riviera Express in the 1930s, so nicknamed because of the large windows, unusual then in British compartment stock (Plate 26).

The models of freight wagons are more numerous and diverse; and that is fortunate, for goods vehicles are at present less well represented in the Museum, though a number of important examples are in store, awaiting restoration and display. The series here gives a good general idea of the evolution of the railways' methods of conveying freight of all kinds, from the primitive coal wagon (two full-sized original examples of which are to be seen outside) to a cement wagon of 1973. One thing in particular can be observed here, better than anywhere else in the Museum, and it is often insufficiently appreciated. The railway was a general carrier, obliged to convey whatever traffic presented itself, unless that was physically impossible owing to the loading gauge – it could hardly be compelled to carry a full-sized giraffe. The extraordinary range of vehicles shown here indicates this compactly. They were built specially for individual sorts of traffic: for carrying coal and bricks (Plate 33) and limestone, meat and fish. In our own time much of the railways' freight traffic goes by containers. Something of that appears here too; it is carried further in the elaborate model of a Freightliner terminal upstairs in the Long Gallery (Case 119).

The Victorian railways in Britain developed freight vehicles markedly different from those to be seen on the Continent, still more from those in the United States, especially in two ways: the majority of them were open wagons, whereas elsewhere they were usually covered in ('box cars' in America); and they were small. The characteristic British unit for many years was the 10-ton open wagon, with a body built wholly of timber. There is an excellent model of one of them here, of the end of the nineteenth century. By that time the British railways were being much criticised for clinging to this practice, and some of them were drawing away from it: see the series of North Eastern Railway coal wagons dating from 1907 to 1920 and varying in capacity from 14 tons to 23. The argument was more complex than it appeared to be. If the unit was uneconomically small, that was in part due to the nature of the business the British railways were called upon to handle and the demands that traders and manufacturers made upon them. Two other things must also be remembered, and both are exemplified here. A large number of the goods vehicles (about half of those running in Britain in 1918) were owned not by railway companies at all but by the private firms that were their customers; and provided they were mechanically sound the railways had no power to force them to adopt different ones. Nearly all goods vehicles were loose-coupled, not fitted with continuous brakes. Hence the low speeds at which British goods trains ran, impeding the general flow of traffic; they could not be operated faster in safety, when the only brake power was that on the engine and the brake van, unless the train was halted (at the head of a steep incline, for example) and the brakes on individual wagons were pinned down by hand. Here was a very serious technical backwardness on British railways–perhaps indeed the weakest point in their equipment. It was left to the nationalised corporation to take up the remedying of it, at a very heavy expenditure, from 1955 onwards.

Between the carriage and the wagon models are two cases containing models of early bridges. All but one are of timber structures –though timber very early became the least characteristic material used by railways for this purpose. They begin with a simple bridge on the Newcastle & Carlisle Railway (which was not originally intended to be worked by locomotives) and proceed to the much more elaborate structure of William Cubitt for the Great Northern Railway at Bardney and two of the longest and most famous series of all timber railway bridges in Britain: those designed by I.K.Brunel for the Great Western Railway and others associated with it in the West Country and South Wales. This pair has been well selected. One is the first of the whole long sequence, a bridge built in 1840 to carry a road over the railway in the deep Sonning cutting. The other is one of the most complex: the Landore viaduct, just outside Swansea, completed ten years later. The model is of the central section of a much larger structure, a third of a mile long; there were thirty-seven bays in all, and it was curved. Frail, even primitive, as these bridges may look, they were designed in this way for good reasons, mainly economic, and the craftsmanship in them was superb. The Landore viaduct was reconstructed in iron in the 1880s, but many stood much longer. The last of them, near Aberdare, was not demolished until 1947.

Next to this model is another of a single span of the High Level Bridge at Newcastle, opened in 1849 and still heavily used today. It was a most advanced structure, of iron on masonry piers, providing for three lines of track and combining the railway on the upper deck with a road on the lower: a dual arrangement that might perhaps have been adopted more widely in later times than it has been. This is one of Robert Stephenson's masterpieces.

The story of railway bridge-building is taken further in the description and pictures placed at the back, which here again are most satisfactory. It extends also to a model of part of the steel Forth Bridge in the Long Gallery (Case 90), and to the original Gaunless Bridge, described on p. 46. But bridges are only one element in civil engineering; and it must be confessed that the others are at present little treated in the Museum.

Behind and above these cases of models, on the back and side walls, are a long series of miscellaneous exhibits, chiefly metal plates of many sizes, shapes, and colours. They constitute an extended and intriguing puzzle; for the Museum has decided here to allow the visitor a rest from instruction and to leave him to make out what they are, and where they came from, himself. Broadly they fall into three groups, ranged from left to right. First a series of headboards (the old term is permissible, even though these are all of metal), carried on the front of a locomotive hauling a named express. They recall some very famous trains: the Cornish Riviera Express, instituted in 1904 and still running; the Cheltenham Flyer, which at one time claimed to be the fastest train in the world; the Irish Mail, whose ancestor began to be known by that title in 1848, which makes it the oldest of all named trains. Below them stands a set of relics of the Jersey Railway, closed down in 1937.

Then comes a long run of nameplates from locomotives – a hundred of them altogether. On some railways such as the Great Western it was the practice for many years to give the engines names only, like ships; others used nothing but numbers. The practice takes one into some curious byways of railway history. Who chose the names, and why – with what purpose in mind? Sometimes they have an obvious source. A number of railways named locomotives after places they served. The Brighton Company's *Boxhill* is an example, and here are nameplates of this sort from other railways – *Tenterden, Ventnor, Greenore*. Some engines were named after members of the royal family or territorial magnates (*Earl of Mount Edgcumbe, Duke of Sutherland*) or local officers of the railway, like *A. S. Harris* of the Plymouth Devonport & South Western Junction. Others have names that reach far back into history. Some were taken from warships; the London & North Western had a splendid series of them, and the tradition was carried on in the 1930s by the LMS Company in *Warspite* and *Agamemnon*. *Novelty* refers us back to an experimental engine at the Rainhill trials; here are *Hackworth* and *Sir Vincent Raven* and half-a-dozen other engineers. The old British Empire (so lately vanished) makes its presence felt too (*Hindostan*,

Bombay, Straits Settlements); and the country's wars, from *Crimea* to *Spitfire*. What a slice of history this is! The right-hand series of plates is quite miscellaneous – station signs, notice boards, lineside indications (Plate 42). In the variety of styles alone they provide a whole course in design. Look for instance at two station boards, Welnetham (Suffolk) and Saddleworth (Yorkshire), the elaborate lining out of the one, the fancy lettering of the other. One of the notices is in Welsh and one bilingual. A much-darkened board gives regulations for the cab-stand at Bakewell station. Another, which will be remembered well in its original place by some visitors, explains the semaphores controlling road traffic at a crossing in Worcester. There is a famous notice to prohibit 'skylarking' among cab-drivers on the South Eastern & Chatham Railway. Some of the companies named are obscure: where did their lines run – the Methley Branch Railway, the North Lindsey Light? Some initials need decoding, like DNG for Dundalk Newry & Greenore. One modern plate brings us home here again. 'Railway Street' is from York itself. About 1846 a new street was called 'Hudson Street', with the concurrence of the great man himself, who had been Lord Mayor of the city (cf. p. 4). In 1852, after his financial crash, that name was altered to 'Railway Street'. Then, in 1971, the original name was restored, and this plate very appropriately rests here.

———

The Main Hall is dominated – like the whole Museum – by the machines that moved on the railway. Naturally, for it was mechanical traction that first gave the railway its superiority over its competitors, and has remained its hallmark ever since. But traction and machines do not constitute the whole. When a railway has been built, its locomotives and carriages and wagons acquired, it has to be run, and it soon becomes a complex organism, managed by its own techniques and controlled by a special kind of discipline. At this point we break away from moving machines to consider methods of operation, devices for ensuring safety, and finally the track on which the trains ran.

They are not treated extensively here; a critic may well say, not extensively enough. But the exhibition is tightly packed, and includes some things essential to an understanding of the way railways were made to work.

First comes a series of the devices employed for regulating traffic out of its normal course: the badges worn by pilotmen, the linesmen's boards to be hung by signalmen out of their boxes when they needed assistance, to repair something that had broken down. Fog presented the railways with some of their greatest difficulties; greater than we appreciate today, when thick fog has become an uncommon event. The detonator, a small cap clipped to the track, containing an explosive and set off with a bang when a wheel ran over it, was invented about 1840 and soon came into general use. Here is one, together with a fogman's lamp and a repeater, for giving a second indication from a semaphore signal that the fog hid from sight.

That brings us to signals. First a set of models, showing their evolution from the early boards and discs to the semaphores that became standard on all British railways until they began to employ colour-light systems from the 1920s onwards. The different patterns of semaphore are shown, though there is not space to demonstrate the full range of variety in their design and detail. One thing is evident from the models: the British practice of making the signal fall downwards to indicate 'all clear'. On some railways – the North Eastern, for instance – a three-position system was used, with the arm at horizontal to indicate 'stop', pointing 45 degrees downwards for 'caution', and falling into a slot in the post out of sight for 'all clear'. Presently it came to be felt that in all circumstances a positive indication should invariably be given, and the two-position practice was adopted. It is shown close by, full size, on a Midland Railway signal fixed by the door into the garden, and in the Great Northern somersault signal outside at the other end (see p. 46). The Americans and others preferred to make the arm rise into the 'upper quadrant', believing it to give a clearer indication; that was the term used there, whilst 'lower quadrant' denoted the British system. In the inter-war years three of the four British companies changed to the upper-quadrant pattern; the fourth, the Great Western, adhered firmly to the established British practice (but see p. 45).

To read these signals rightly – numerous and complicated at large junctions – required intelligence on the part of the drivers, and good eyesight. Their eyes were tested in a number of ways, both for distant vision and for discrimination between colours, for colour-blindness is a defect by no means uncommon. Here are two simple pieces of apparatus used for this purpose.

Signalling came to depend in large measure on the electric telegraph (see also p. 36), and later on the telephone. The block system, first developed in Britain – and a cause of admiration even to Americans, who otherwise thought their own railways much superior – would have been impracticable without the telegraph. It is well explained, in a concise fashion, on one of the back panels here. Some telegraph and telephone instruments are shown, together with a number of varieties of repeaters installed in signal-boxes to help the signalman when the semaphore he was controlling was beyond his sight, too far away or round a curve. Other forms of visual aid are also shown: the discs carried at the front of the train on some railways–especially those with a very dense service into and out of London, like the Great Eastern and the Brighton–to indicate the nature of the train or its route; tail boards, used to show that a train was following.

Between the cases containing these small objects stands a full-sized signalling installation, exemplifying British practice in the 1930s. Two lever frames, of different patterns, are placed one at each end. The whole apparatus is in working order and is used for demonstration.

On the other side of the door is one more group of exhibits. It is a small group, yet in some respects the most fundamentally important in the Museum, for it is concerned with the track, the 'rail way' that was the first distinguishing feature of this means of transport. However important such material may be, it is not easy to show it intelligibly. Most railway museums, in this country and abroad, have failed this test. Here the challenge has been met, and successfully. A clear story emerges, an evolution is demonstrated.

It begins with a pair of timber rails from Groverake mine in County Durham, dating perhaps from the middle of the eighteenth century, and passes to a section of the iron rack rail used with Blenkinsop's loco-motives at Leeds (see p. 45). Then comes a rail from the Stockton & Darlington: fish-bellied in shape underneath and laid on stone blocks. From this point, through the Liverpool & Manchester, the development towards the modern forms becomes clear, though with a proper atten-tion to some variants, such as Brunel's used on the Great Western Rail-way and W.H.Barlow's, patented in 1849, which had the merit of dispensing with sleepers altogether and so was cheap in first cost. There are other elements in the track besides rails and sleepers, and some of them are shown here too: the fishplate, patented two years before by William Bridges Adams and Robert Richardson, chairs, and crossing devices. So we come towards our own time, with the electric track circuit and the modern version of the flat-bottomed rail fastened directly to the sleeper, of timber or concrete, a pattern that has come to be adopted even in Britain, which had clung tenaciously to its established practice of carrying the rail in chairs. Finally, two items of lineside furniture: a

boundary stone indicating the limits of the property of the York &
North Midland Railway, and a set of mileposts of the pattern peculiar
to the North Eastern (Plate 37).

The descriptions here are admirable, and keyed in well to the exhibits
themselves. More could be said, and demonstrated too, if there were
more room; but what is offered is a thoroughly efficient exposition of the
main elements in the story of railway track in Britain.

3
The Long Gallery

From this point, close to the track exhibits, a staircase leads up to the Long Gallery. It is long indeed, and it contains the principal exhibition concerned with British railways in general – not primarily with their mechanical equipment, which is shown in the other parts of the Museum, but with their history and work in the broadest sense. It divides into two main sections. The first, starting at the head of the staircase, surveys the history in one continuous story, down to the present day. The second part is given up to the old companies, as they were before nationalisation; and it ends with a small section on railway steamships.

We begin with the prehistory of railways: their origins in connection with mining, when traffic on them was confined to coal and moved entirely by horses and men. The railway's rivals also appear here, the canal and the horse-drawn coach. With mechanical traction, developed fully on the Stockton & Darlington and Liverpool & Manchester lines, the modern railway arrives. Something of the curiosity and excitement it aroused is conveyed here, for example by the medals and pieces of commemorative pottery produced to celebrate the railways' opening (Plates 48–9). A large diorama of Euston station stands on its own: particularly informative because it shows it at a very early stage, in the mid-1840s, before the Great Hall and offices had been built, and gives a good idea of the original surroundings of the station, when London came to an end at Euston Square and Camden Town was a detached suburb. Among the early railway literature displayed here, notice the advertisements of the Newcastle & Carlisle Company. There is a long series of them (only a few are shown, but there are many more in the collection: announcing special trains to Stagshawbank Fair and Carlisle Races, sea trips to the Isle of Man and Dublin.

A series of well-designed graphics demonstrates the growth of the railway system and of the work it performed: the number of passengers carried, the development of freight business, the reduction in time taken on journeys. Slides, many of them in colour, on automatic projection depict special topics: the growth of commuting and holiday traffic, for example. A particularly good feature is a pair of maps, one showing the physical extension of the system in each decade from 1830 to 1860, the other the chief lines of each of the principal companies as they were established before 1923. The amount of work involved in preparing the material for these, and the difficulties of presenting them clearly, will be appreciated only by those who have struggled with making complicated railway maps themselves.

One consequence of the spread of railways, which has often been remarked on but never analysed as fully as it should have been, was the adoption of a uniform system of time throughout the country, taken from Greenwich. It was often called 'railway time'; it appears as such on the face of a clock here, made in York (Plate 44). The cardinal importance of accurate time, both in running trains and in maintaining railway discipline, is symbolised by the timepieces and watches issued by the companies to their guards and other servants; a number of them are exhibited here.

The development of standard time was aided by the electric telegraph, which owed its early development to the alliance it formed with the railway. It owed something too to a celebrated sensation, a murder case in 1845, when the criminal's rapid arrest was due to the use of the new instrument. Here is a handbill advertising admission to the telegraph offices at Paddington and Slough, to a public curious to see how the feat had been achieved.

The early arrangements for booking passengers at stations were leisurely and cumbrous. They evolved from the stage coaches and were hand-written, except where metal tokens were employed, as they were by the London & Greenwich Railway. Such methods were soon superseded through the ingenuity of Thomas Edmondson, who invented first a dating and then a printing press in 1837–39 for use on the small rectangular pieces of cardboard that remained standard on all British railways until nationalisation. Specimens of Edmondson's presses are shown in the Gallery, with a substantial number of the tickets that evolved from his work – even one issued for a ferry journey in the USSR, on Lake Baykal: besides some others from foreign railways, showing designs and techniques different from his. The tickets displayed here, from the Museum's extensive collection, indicate some of the different styles of printing adopted by the various companies; note for instance the large figures overprinted on those of the North London Railway, a device for enabling the collectors to identify destinations quickly on that densely-used system. The tickets issued for special kinds of travellers, and the articles that passengers took with them, are interesting (see plate 52). They range from one for a circular tour from Manchester through Connemara to a ticket for the conveyance of a fowl on the East African Railways bearing a picture of the bird, no doubt to help an illiterate passenger. There are a number of Parliamentary tickets, issued at a penny a mile under the terms of the Railway Regulation Act of 1844, and at the other end of the scale of comfort, a first-class sleeping car ticket from King's Cross to Berwick and stations beyond.

The day-to-day life of the railway is reflected in some of the pieces of equipment carried by railwaymen: the engine-driver's oil-can and his lamp for inspecting the dark parts of his machine, the pay-tin for wages, the brass megaphone for calling out orders; the trade-union badges, the ceremonial sash of an official of the National Union of Railwaymen. These are balanced by the ordinary equipment of passengers. Here for instance are one or two of the little lamps they used to supplement the feeble oil illumination provided in railway carriages until the 1880s – and often later than that (Plate 51); and a footwarmer, for steam heating did not become general even on main-line trains until about the same time, and these heated tins, covered in carpet, had not altogether disappeared in the 1920s (Plate 50). There is a handsome gentleman's sandwich box for refreshment on the journey; the lunch basket, supplied by the railway, only begins to appear in Britain in 1875, the restaurant car in 1879.

The impact of the two World Wars on the railways is variously illustrated: by mugs from soldiers' canteens on railway stations (Plate 55), by a photograph of one of Gresley's Pacific locomotives wrecked by a bomb in 1942 inside this very building; by the medal instituted by the LNER for acts of gallantry performed by its men (Plate 56). It was sometimes gallantry of the highest order; the George Cross won by Driver Axon in 1957 is now in the Museum.

That leads us to nationalisation and to some of the developments it has brought. The next section is called 'The Modern Image', and it illustrates the continuous flow of history from yesterday into today, with even a glance at tomorrow. We are reminded again of the APT, demonstrated more completely downstairs; and here is a model of the HST, the High Speed Train (Inter-City 125), diesel-powered and more conventional, which has put Britain back into the international top league of express train operation once more. The large and excellent model of a Freightliner terminal shows something of the new methods of handling traffic by containers (Plate 39). The underground railways in London – which have played a distinguished part in the development of the British railway system and are scarcely noticed anywhere else in the Museum – appear here with a good working model of the type of tunnelling shield used in constructing the Victoria Line (Plate 38) and a cross section of two of its tunnels to illustrate different methods of lining them; as well as a demonstration of the Metalastik rubber springs used in the bogies of the vehicles running on that line and on the underground railway in Stockholm.

At this point the first section ends, and the exhibition is broken into by a small theatre, providing continuous slide shows. It is resumed on the other side, first with a delightful group of 'Toys and Treasures', including some crude early model trains, a board game for children, a baby's bowl and a railway alphabet, and a very complete model of a station (Plate 58); evidence of the impact made by the Victorian railway on the minds of children and adults alike.

This leads into the treatment of the private companies, from the Stockton & Darlington to the four big ones of 1923–47. It is frankly a miscellany, unsystematic, ultimately impressionistic if you like; and so must this account be too. Everyone will pick out what takes his fancy, or hers. The range of interest is wide. Let me offer a few examples of things that seem to me worth looking for, not exactly in the order in which they are shown.

There are again tickets – the indicators of journeys made; but different from those further back. All railway companies issued free passes, to their directors and senior servants, who necessarily travelled much on their systems in the course of business. They came in all shapes and sizes and materials, ivory and leather as well as metal. A few even bore the name of the holder embossed or engraved on them, like Sir Ralph Wedgwood's from the London & North Eastern Railway. From the North British comes a strip of tickets, in four parts, for a railway and steamer trip from Cowlairs to Tighnabruaich. There are also cards of admission to the special display put on by the North Eastern Company in 1875 at Darlington to commemorate the fiftieth anniversary of the opening of the Stockton & Darlington Railway.

The crockery, cutlery, and glass from refreshment rooms, dining cars, and railway steamships offer a good panoramic view of British commercial art (Plates 41, 46–7). Much of it is robust and heavy, as it had to be in constant and rough service; sometimes handsome as well. This applies particularly to things used on railway ships: the massive teapot from the Great Central steamer *Wrexham*, the blue-and-white crockery from ships connected with the London Brighton & South Coast Railway. On the other hand there are some things here that are more delicate, even elegant: the pretty cups and plates of the London & North Eastern Company, for instance, the little white bowl on a stem from the Lancashire & Yorkshire, announcing that it contained 'cane sugar from Demarara, British Guiana'. (Was that to proclaim the high quality of what was offered, or does it show a lingering desire to prove that the sugar had not been produced by slaves – something that many Manchester Liberals, in particular, would be glad to know?) Some older refinements of manners are represented here too: by the grape-scissors from the Great Eastern, the Manchester Sheffield & Lincolnshire crumb-scoop, and the clothes-brush provided by the London & South Western. Finally, one delightful little treasure: the metal snuff-box given to Mr M.McDonald by the staff of the station at Woodside, near Aberdeen, on the Great North of Scotland Railway at its opening in 1854.

There are seven models of railway ships, and it must be admitted that at present they are crowded together and rather unsympathetically treated. This is one of the few points at which someone familiar with the Museum of British Transport at Clapham is likely to feel that a display was better handled there. At York they are simply placed in pairs, one above another – almost as if they were asleep in bunks – without any attempt at all to suggest that their element was water. Two are of paddle steamers of the Mid-Victorian age: *Rose* from the Irish Sea, *Mary Beatrice* from the English Channel. The rest all belong to the inter-war years. Two are early car ferries: *Autocarrier*, the first to be specially built for service in the Channel, and *Lymington*, which plied to and from the Isle of Wight (Plate 40). *Dinard* was one of the earliest ships commissioned by the new Southern Railway in 1924, to run from Southampton to St Malo. The finest of the series is perhaps *Duke of Lancaster*; the second ship of that name, built for the Heysham – Belfast run by the London Midland & Scottish Company in 1928. Something of the comfort it provided, at its most expensive, is shown in the model of the *de luxe* cabins that appears alongside.

Each of these ships had its own history, no less than the locomotives below, and it would be useful to have it summarised here. *Duke of Lancaster*, for example, was accident-prone. In 1931 she was burnt and sank in Heysham Harbour, to be salvaged two months afterwards; altogether she was in seven mishaps between 1928 and 1940. *Dinard* had a long history. She became a hospital ship in the second War, served at Dunkirk, was mined in the invasion of Normandy, was turned into a car ferry and plied between Folkestone and Boulogne until 1958. Thereupon the Finns bought her, renamed her *Viking* and set her to cross from Finland to Sweden.

It seems a pity that the series ends at this point, except for a hover-craft, awkwardly displayed in a case some distance away; for there is a 'modern image' in the sea services of British Railways too.

The Long Gallery contains about three-fifths of all the objects shown in the Museum. In a few pages only a very small sample can be picked out for mention. But even this highly selective treatment should indicate something of the variety to be found here, the solid information, the appearance occasionally of the unexpected. Most visitors will find something to interest them, whatever their tastes and ideas. For some it will be the most enthralling part of the whole Museum.

1 The Railway Museum, Queen Street, York (1927–73)

2 The Museum of British Transport, Clapham (1961–73)

3 York old station in 1960; the city wall on the left

4 The motive-power depot before its conversion into the Museum

Two views of the move to York (see p 4):

5 By Elstow brick-works, south of Bedford

6 At Sundon, north of Luton, 19 November 1977

7 The entrance to the Museum

8 Inside the Museum: locomotives facing their turntable

9 The sectioned locomotive, *Ellerman Lines* (see p 7)

10 *Gladstone*, dressed in honour of the Silver Jubilee in 1977

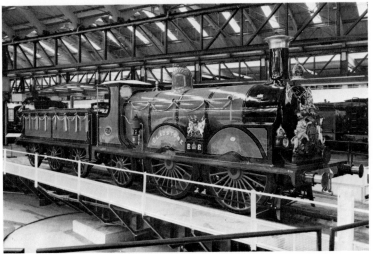

11 South Eastern & Chatham Railway No. 737 on the inspection pit

12 *Coppernob* of the Furness Railway (see p 15)

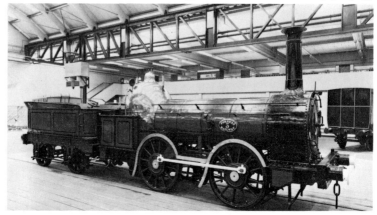

13 Great Eastern Railway No. 87 (see p 13)

14 Model of Grand Junction Railway locomotive *Wildfire* made by John Stagg of Birmingham in 1839: one of the oldest locomotive models in existence

15 North Eastern Railway No. 1961 (see p 15): the model in its case

16 The diesel shunter and *Evening Star* (see pp 18–19) standing outside the Museum; the towers of the Minster in the background

17 North Eastern Railway electric locomotive of 1904 (see p 18)

18 British Railways diesel-electric locomotive (1957): present class 31

The Museum's locomotives in action.

19 Great Northern Railway No. 1 at speed on one of her special runs in 1938

20 *Hardwicke* and the Midland compound ready to start at Carnforth, 1976

21 Stockton & Darlington Railway carriage of the 1840s

22 North Eastern Railway dynamometer car (see p 22)

23 Midland Railway carriage (see p 22) with some of those responsible for its restoration in the British Railways workshops at Wolverton

24 Postal sorting carriage built by the London & North Western Railway. The net for picking up mails *en route* is at the side. The vehicle is fitted with Webb's radial trucks (see p 22)

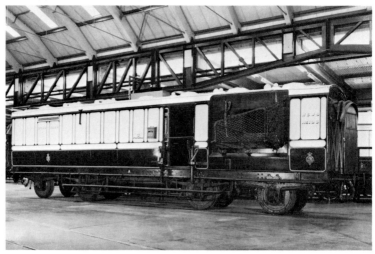

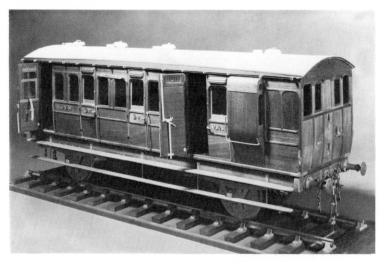

25 Model of Great Eastern Railway third-class carriage

26 The modeller's realism: interior of compartment in the Great Western
    Railway 'Sunshine' coach (see p 28)

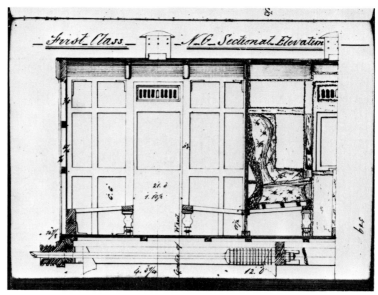

27 Drawing from a notebook of Sir Daniel Gooch, showing design for a first-class carriage, Great Western Railway (standard gauge)

28 Pullman car *Topaz* (see p 23)

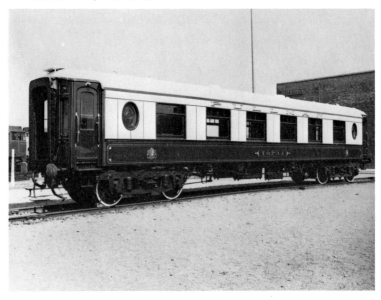

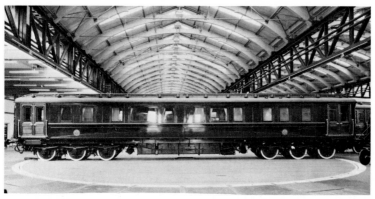

29 King Edward VII's saloon standing on the second turntable across the
Main Hall

30 Interior of the day room in Queen Victoria's saloon (see p 24)

31 Wagon and track from Peak Forest tramroad

32 The Gaunless Bridge, with chaldron wagon standing on it (see p 46)

33 Model of Great Northern Railway brick wagon

34 Model of private owner's wagon

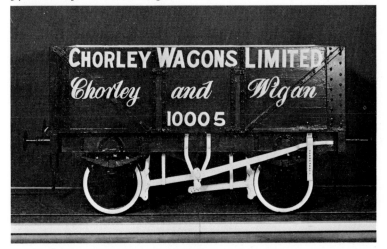

35 Oil wagon, 1889

37 North Eastern Railway mileposts, and part of the display of track

38 Model of tunnelling shield used in construction of the Victoria line, London Transport, in the 1960s

36 Wooden lathe used by George Stephenson, from Killingworth

39 Model of Freightliner terminal

40 Model of Southern Railway car-ferry *Lymington* (1938), replacing a service by tow-boat and barge between Lymington and Yarmouth (I o w)

41 A piece of ship's crockery

42 Group of station nameboards and notices at the back of the Main Hall

43

44

43 The Front Gallery. Restaurant-car conductor in the centre; back left, model of Liverpool & Manchester Railway carriage; right, the *épergne* presented to Robert Stephenson (see p 42)

44 Clock made in York showing 'railway time' – i.e. Greenwich time, which the railways made standard throughout the country

45 Figure of a navvy in the Long Gallery

46

47

48

46 Cutlery used in railway
   hotels, refreshment rooms,
   and restaurant-cars

47 Great Central Railway
   coffee-pot

48 Mug to commemorate the
   Rainhill trials of 1829, depicting
   one of the competing
   locomotives, *Novelty*

49 Medal commemorating the
   opening of the Liverpool &
   Manchester Railway, 1830;
   the reverse, showing the
   entrance to the tunnel at
   Liverpool

49

50

51

ELECTRIC READING LAMP.
PUT PENNY in SLOT
PRESS KNOB HARD.
Small Knob Extinguishes

50 Footwarmer for use in railway carriage

51 Penny-in-the-slot reading lamp installed in railway carriages

52 Three of the Museum's large collection of railway tickets, showing special
concessions given to workers in a variety of industries

53 North Eastern Railway
hand-bell

54 Stationmaster's lamp from
Wolferton, Great Eastern
Railway

54

53

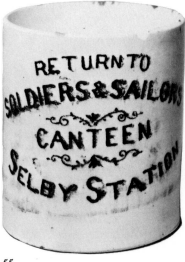

55

56

55 Mug from First World War
canteen

56 London & North Eastern
Railway medal for gallantry in
the Second World War

57 Conductor's tobacco box

57

58 Toy railway station

59 Coat of arms of the North London Railway

60 Seal of the Shropshire Union Company, a unique undertaking promoted
by canal companies to convert their canals into railways

59

60

61 London & North Eastern Railway poster

62 Midland Railway poster. The Company never reached Blackpool itself.
The poster is of about 1890 (before the Tower was built)

63 Portrait of Edward Fletcher, Locomotive Engineer of the North Eastern
Railway, 1854–82 (see p 9)

64 *Farewell to the Light Brigade*: oil painting by Robert Collinson, 1863.
Waterloo station

Four examples of photographs from the Museum's collection:

65 Rugby station, 1896

66 Ancient carriage body in use as a railway workmen's hut

67 Horse-drawn delivery van

68 Accident on the Caledonian Railway

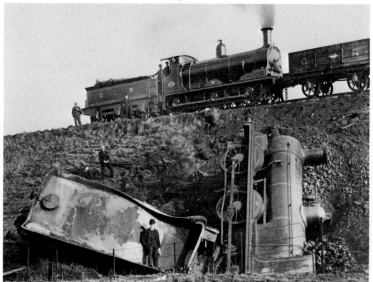

69 Entrance to the Main Hall. *Agenoria* in front (see pp 7–8); statue of George Stephenson by E H Baily behind it; Weatherhill winding-engine at the rear (see p 25)

4
The Front Gallery

The exhibition here is devoted largely to the human life of the railway. Eight railway officials preside over the room, each in his uniform. The figures here are all good, and at their best first-class, excellently placed against photographic backgrounds appropriate to their business. In time they range from a Stockton & Darlington Railway guard of 1860 to a carter, a page, and a restaurant-car conductor of British Railways ninety years later (Plate 43). They appear so convincing because no effort has been made to render them unsuitably animated. Looked at from a little way off, the head porter of the hotel is keeping his eye on a potentially troublesome character, the conductor is making out his bill, the sharp-eyed stationmaster is alert to all that is going on – each of them has been caught, as it were, going about his business.

Three well-known paintings of the interior of railway carriages hang here, from the 1850s and 1860s, together with two concerned with war: Robert Collinson's 'Farewell to the Light Brigade', at Waterloo, and Richard Jack's large 'Return to the Front. Victoria Station' – no work of art indeed, but a document in history. One or two of the other large pictures are more pleasing: the gay arrival of Queen Victoria at King's Cross for York races (much good detail here in the crowd) and J.M. Baynes's large water-colour of the Dinting viaduct, east of Manchester, done in 1846; technologically interesting because it shows very clearly the laminated timber construction. T.C. Dibdin's two unpretending water-colours of the Eastern Counties main line while it was being built in 1838 are charming and informative.

At the far end of the gallery are two large water-colour drawings of the interior of King's Cross goods station; an important novelty when it was brought into use in 1852 because it combined provision at once for rail, road, and water transport. Notice the barges, on a side branch of the Regent's Canal, in the centre of the upper picture. That picture was engraved for the *Illustrated London News* at the time; the other was never reproduced. Who was the artist? Is there a clue in the initials GA and TA painted prominently on a barrel and a bale of goods?

41

Three paintings of locomotives are worth attention here. Two are pieces of folk art, one signed by Michael Bishop and the other probably by him too, of engines on the Midland Railway. The third illustrates a frequent difficulty in interpreting work of this kind. It is a very careful drawing of the Great Western broad-gauge express engine *Tartar* by E.Rees, 'drawn and measured', we are told, to a scale of $\frac{3}{4}$ in = 1 ft. But why should the engine and tender be painted blue, a colour they never bore? The draughtsman may have been trying to render the colour of the unpainted iron, before the familiar Great Western green was applied to it, or the colour may have changed through varied bleaching of mixed pigments in it: we cannot be certain.

Another kind of art is represented by the elaborate illuminated address presented to Sir Henry Oakley at the end of his thirty-four years' chairmanship of the Board of Management of the Railway Benevolent Institution; some of the flower painting, in the border and round the monogram, attains real delicacy. Finally, it is good to see here two of the original oil paintings by Norman Wilkinson for the posters he did for the London Midland & Scottish and London & North Eastern Railways: bold, strong, technically well observed, they show the artist's special feeling for ships. One is of the arrival of a steamer at Holyhead from Ireland, the other of the departure of the Continental steamers on a summer night from Harwich.

Two cases are given up to glass and plate, elaborate and plain. Notice the formidably large metal jug from the St Enoch Hotel in Glasgow, and by contrast the shapely little one from a London & North Western restaurant car. Of the big ceremonial pieces the most conspicuous – indeed overpowering – is the *épergne* presented to Robert Stephenson 'by a numerous body of friends' on the completion of the London & Birmingham Railway in 1839: a very early Victorian piece, showing already much of the undisciplined exuberance we associate with the Great Exhibition of 1851. At the base of the stem note the panel depicting the Wolverton viaduct nearing completion, copied exactly from Bourne's lithograph. There are also here a few of the ceremonial trowels that were customarily presented on the opening of new lines of railway: some coarsely, some delicately engraved.

The central case in the Gallery contains an exceptionally fine model of a Liverpool & Manchester Railways carriage. Across the windows runs a series of panels of stained glass (artistically vile) from the Manchester Sheffield & Lincolnshire Company's works at Gorton; on the inside wall are examples of the armorial bearings of railways companies

– which are illustrated too in the glass-topped cases containing their seals (Plates 59–60).

Of the other miscellaneous objects two may be mentioned in conclusion. One is the beautiful long-case clock of the Oxford Worcester & Wolverhampton Railway, still in excellent working order. The other is the poster advertising the Telegraph Coach. This is a rare piece of evidence for the practice of carrying passengers in a coach mounted on a flat railway truck. Private individuals sometimes chose to be conveyed in this way in their own carriages, though even that practice was not common; and in early days empty mail coaches might be sent like this down the line to its furthest point, and then taken off and put on to the road. Here is evidence, from as late as the 1850s, for such conveyance of passengers within the coach itself; for the poster distinctly promises that they will be taken from Yeovil to Waterloo 'without change of carriage'. The practice must have ceased immediately the railway was opened between Salisbury and Yeovil in 1860.

5
Outdoor Exhibits

The south-east garden, reached through the door by the signalling exhibition, is a small triangular space, grassed and enclosed in brick walls. It contains the Study Coach (see p. 47), an open vehicle of the standard type introduced on to British Railways in the 1950s.

Some other things of note stand around it. Immediately alongside is a very early water-crane from Coventry, built by Bury's firm. One of the small turntables installed for handling carriages at Euston station in the 1830s is also here; and an early wooden coal wagon from South Hetton Colliery, County Durham. The tall signal is a curiosity. At first sight it seems to be an ordinary upper-quadrant (p. 32) pair of semaphores. But it is of Great Western design and construction, and the Great Western stuck to the lower-quadrant pattern to the end of its life, that is down to 1947. This one was installed experimentally just north of Oxford station. Near its foot stands a set of wheels that may come from one of the locomotives built in 1812–13 under John Blenkinsop's patent for the Middleton Colliery Railway at Leeds, with cogs engaging in racks at the side of the rails. The object of this arrangement was to increase the power of the machine. These are among the earliest surviving locomotive wheels of any kind.

One of the great experiments in railway history is also reflected here: in the iron pipe laid on the ground, which comes from the London & Croydon Railway. That was designed to work on the atmospheric principle, i.e. by air power, and indeed it was so worked for fifteen months in 1846–7. The apparatus was then abandoned. One may regret that no means were found of overcoming its deficiencies: for the system provided noiseless travel, free from smoke (except in the vicinity of the pumping stations), and it greatly reduced the weight on the track by eliminating locomotives.

At the other end of the Museum, beside the entrance, there is a second open space, differently managed: not laid down to grass, but a thoroughfare with the car-park adjoining on one side and the main railway lines on another. Here a number of large exhibits have been assembled, one of outstanding importance. This is a section of the Gaunless Bridge, completed in 1823: the first large metal railway bridge ever built. It was not the first of any kind, for a small one had been erected at Robertstown in South Wales in 1811; but that was designed to carry very light traffic only. George Stephenson was responsible for its design, in collaboration with the ironfounders who built it, Burrells of Newcastle. It is constructed of fish-bellied wrought-iron girders, suspended between cast-iron columns. The bridge gave some trouble at first, part of it being washed away in a flood – the Gaunless is a wild stream, in spate during the winter; it was extended and strengthened so effectively that it stood until 1901. Then the North Eastern Railway decided to rebuild it in a modern fashion; but its historic importance was recognised, and commendable pains were taken to dismantle it, so that it could be re-erected in due course elsewhere. Part of the bridge is shown without its decking, to expose some details of the construction, and another early coal wagon stands above. If the Museum is at its weakest in its treatment of the civil engineering of railways, it can claim here a possession of the first rank (Plate 32).

Another signal is to be seen near by; one of the 'somersault' variety developed first on the Great Northern Railway and subsequently on several railways in South Wales, and more improbably in Australia. Four special-purpose wagons are also here: for carrying nitric acid, liquid chlorine, and petrol. The most interesting of them historically is the black one, an early example dating from 1889. Notice that its frame is built entirely of timber; that appears very plainly beneath the drum of the tank (Plate 35).

Whenever you are out here, it will not be long before a train goes by on one of the adjoining lines, and there will be a row of diesel locomotives standing, waiting their turn of service, exactly as (many visitors will remember it) the steam engines used to do twenty years ago: Pacifics and North Eastern 4-6-0s and shunting engines, and their predecessors before them. If you look over the lines beyond, there is the massive bulk of the Minster. In this Museum, at every turn, the past and the present mingle.

6
The Museum's Services

Museums should not be judged solely on their public display. For some, indeed, this is hardly more than the tip of an iceberg; so much of their work goes on under the surface, behind the scenes. It would not be true to say just that of the National Railway Museum, or of any museum whose visitors are numbered in millions, for the great majority of those visitors must be attracted by what they come to see for themselves. Nevertheless, other things here are very important besides the display, and something must be said of them now.

Two of them are public, for everyone to see and use: the shop and the refreshment room. The shop is basically a bookshop, but it sells a large variety of goods: books large and small, maps, photographs, souvenirs of all kinds. It has been very popular from the day of opening, demanding more space than it was allocated. New premises have therefore had to be built for it, and this has allowed the refreshment room–also heavily patronised–to be extended as well.

Every good museum must be, in a broad sense, an educational institution. This one bears that character strongly, in intention and performance. It receives very large numbers of school parties, coming not from Yorkshire alone but from all over the country. The Museum was planned and equipped from the outset with this need in mind. Here it had the great advantage of springing from the Science Museum, which has devoted itself to such visitors especially for many years and handles a larger number of them than any other museum in Britain. The Education Officer and his Assistant at York can afford much help to visiting school parties: a guided tour of a section of the Museum, for example, a talk of half-an-hour or more in the Lecture Theatre, special lectures and film shows. They can also assist teachers in preparing for their visits. While parties are at the Museum they can have the use of the Study Coach that has been installed in the garden for their work, and in the middle of the day for eating lunch.

On every day in the year during term-time some parties of this sort will be seen in the Museum; they are often more conspicuous than

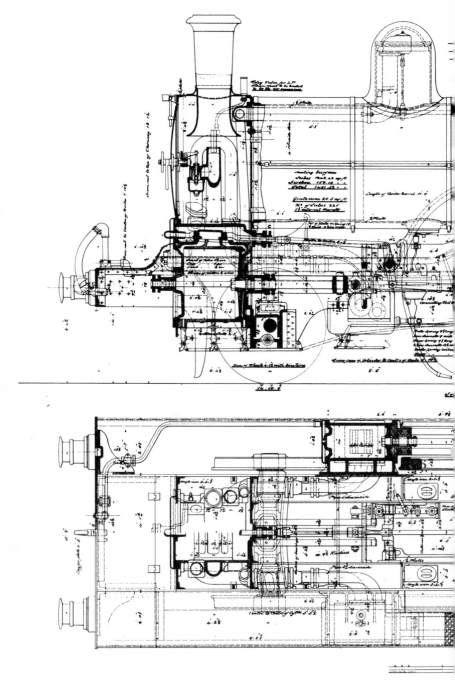

One of the Museum's collection of mechanical engineering drawings: Webb's compound locomotive *Jeanie Deans* (see p 51), signed by Webb himself, 1890

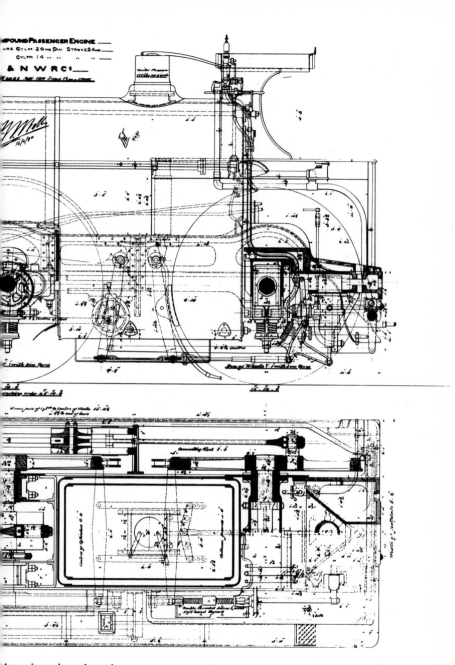

7ᵗ COMPOUND PASSENGER ENGINE.

visitors of any other description. It is interesting to observe the widely different activities of the children themselves, their reactions to what they look at and learn. To take only one example: many of them draw pictures of the things they are shown, and an interesting selection of these drawings and paintings is usually exhibited in the Museum, together with some models. All the things included were done by children under sixteen. Some of them showed close and perceptive attention to details of the machines they depicted; others a refreshing impressionism, suggesting some of the directions in which the mind and eye might take off from plain reality.

But the educational work of the Museum is not limited to young schoolchildren. From its very nature it sets out to communicate with a broad range of people of all ages, to spread knowledge and increase understanding of railways, in terms of technology and history, in the past and right down to the present day. The Museum is keen to demonstrate what is going on now, and to make projections into the future. That is all part of the continuity of history: one of the most important demonstrations that the Museum offers, as well as its reconstruction of the distant past. Such a presentation is educational in the widest sense. It places technology in its proper context.

To keep abreast of all these developments, with current railway practice and with the continuing growth of historical knowledge, a library is essential on the spot, and this the Museum has set out to assemble. It has been working here with only a small previous foundation to build on, and a good library is the work of many years. Already, however, this one is a useful instrument, constantly in use by the staff of the Museum and available (though only by previous appointment with the Librarian) to members of the public. If the working space is limited, it is good. It is agreeable to have at one's disposal here a majestic desk that is reputed to have belonged to Robert Stephenson.

The Library has another function as well. It serves as a centre of information on all the subjects within the scope of the Museum, and it has already built up a well-established reputation for this service.

The holdings of the Library are not confined to books and periodicals. In its care are the very important collections of photographs and engineering drawings, mechanical and civil. There are some 80,000 glass negatives here already, and the number is constantly growing. They cover all aspects of railway work: from machines and equipment to buildings and engineering works, and then to the life of the railway, caught formally and informally by the camera (Plates 65–8). There is a photographic studio in the Museum for printing and copying work.

The engineering drawings number about 100,000: a vast assemblage, many of them in poor condition when received, uncatalogued and unidentified. It has been an important task for the Museum to sort, list, and repair these, making them available for study, and that work proceeds steadily. It will take a long time to complete; and by then, no doubt, there will be thousands more drawings awaiting attention. For an example see pp. 48–9.

Side by side with them may be mentioned the Museum's fine collection of railway posters (Plates 61–2). This includes not only the printed versions displayed at stations and on boardings, but also a considerable number of the artists' original paintings.

One other activity must also be mentioned: among the most important of all, yet proceeding as a rule quite unseen by the public. The machines and other objects in the Museum need constant care and attention. They often arrive in poor condition, rusty, unpainted, lacking essential parts of their equipment. In that state they demand restoration; and when restored they must be satisfactorily maintained. 'Restoration' is itself a term of controversy, often involving delicate and difficult decisions. Locomotives, for example, seldom remained entirely unaltered throughout their working lives. When one comes to be preserved, should it be kept exactly as it was when taken out of service, or should it go back as far as possible to its original condition? There is no single rule to be followed here: each case has to be considered carefully on its own. That is a task for the Keeper and his colleagues, drawing when necessary on the best advice available. And then the work has to be executed, to a precise specification, either inside the Museum or outside.

The greater part of this work, and all day-to-day maintenance, is carried out in the Museum. It has workshops well equipped for the purpose and a highly skilled staff. The problems to be dealt with are diverse, and solutions have often to be worked out experimentally. The properties of paint for instance, the ways in which it is affected by temperature and humidity, the character of pigments and the resulting colours – all these need the closest study. You will sometimes hear a railway enthusiast exclaim that this or that locomotive has been painted in a green (even in a black) of a wrong shade. He may be right; and yet the original specification may have been followed as exactly as modern paint will allow. Or – equally – he may be wrong: for such judgments are in part subjective, and two people, both experienced, will often see the same colour differently. It is very important to get such a matter as nearly right as possible. In museum conditions a railway vehicle should be able to last without repainting for twenty years.

The problems of maintenance are of course greatly increased with locomotives that are used in service. The Museum has played an important part in the recent revival of steam traction, and continues to do so; but this has required a great deal of time and effort, from a staff strictly limited in numbers. It has been a fine sight to see *Hardwicke* or the Midland compound with steam up outside the Museum (Plate 20). Not many of those who enjoy the sight realise how many man-hours it has demanded, or the thought and skill that the operation may have involved.

That work is one of the signs of the close relationship between the Museum and the railway preservation movement, which has been a feature of British life over the past thirty years. The movement began with the successful effort made on behalf of the Talyllyn Railway in 1950–51; it grew slowly, tentatively at first and in the face of some ridicule. Not all the ridicule was misplaced: some of the plans put forward had their absurdities, aiming at the preservation or rescue of lines that never had the smallest chance of proving themselves, showing ludicrous notions about engineering and economics and the law. But the movement generated gradually a real strength too, raising and maintaining enthusiasm, which was often put to hard tests: of finding cash quickly, not from the rich but from people who had to think carefully about pounds and pence, of undertaking heavy and unpleasant physical labour, often on Saturdays and Sundays on top of the week's work. One who observed all this without being directly involved in it may pay his tribute of admiration to the result. There are today over 100 miles of railway in England and Wales that have been rescued from closure and brought back into use with difficulty, after long neglect. A total of more than 600 steam locomotives are preserved, some of them at major centres like Didcot, Hereford, and Carnforth, others singly, standing as lone monuments sometimes in unlikely places – Tiverton, Corby, Stafford, Dunfermline.

The National Railway Museum itself, and its predecessor at Clapham, are partly to be seen as a product of this movement. The enthusiasm expressed for the railway, and especially for the steam locomotive, by the preservationists did much to make the case for founding and maintaining them. As the national museum devoted to the subject, and as a daughter of the Science Museum (whose railway collections reach back over more than a century and include some of the most truly historic machines in the world), this Museum has an important part to play as a link between the many bodies and persons involved in railway preservation of all kinds up and down the country; sometimes as a co-ordinator of activity, a counsellor and friend, always as a centre for information. It also maintains close relations with British Railways. That is important, and not something to be taken simply for granted. The business of the staff of BR is to make the system work, as efficiently as they can, for the service of the community. The past history of that system, the machines that have become obsolete in working it, do not concern them directly. At times indeed those things have appeared to be troublesome lumber, impeding the work of modernisation, of planning for the future. Yet a sense of pride in the long continuity of railways in Britain still continues in the nationalised corporation. It shows that sense constantly in its friendly relationship with the Museum at York.

The Museum has moreover a foot in the world outside Britain, taking its share in the work of the International Association of Transport Museums, and of other co-operative bodies of that kind. This is a function that must always have a peculiar importance because of the unique part that Britain played in the establishment and early development of the mechanically-operated railway.

A visitor who sits down to rest (perhaps on one of the numerous railway-station seats provided in the Main Hall) on his way round the Museum, or who looks back on his visit afterwards, may well care to think of all this activity, which continues endlessly behind the scenes at York.

A museum is the product of many minds: of the people who work to establish it in the first place, who plan its accommodation and display and decide what it is to include. It owes a debt beyond acknowledgment to all those who preserved the things it contains; very often, in a museum like this one, to their foresight in saving from the scrap-heap things that had been discarded and seemed of no value. It also embodies the experience, the ingenuity and skill of those who designed and made the objects themselves.

One great man presides here–perhaps, in the end, the greatest of all railway engineers: George Stephenson. E.H.Baily's statue of him, which once stood at Euston station, is the first thing inside the Museum that the visitor sees, looking straight ahead as he arrives (Plate 69). It rears up, at its full colossal height, by the entrance to the Main Hall. A little way off is the wooden lathe used at Killingworth in the construction of his earliest locomotives (Plate 36). The Gaunless Bridge outside represents a technical experiment hardly less remarkable than *Rocket*. At the opposite end of the Hall, in the garden, stands the bronze memorial to Stephenson, subscribed for by Italian railwaymen in 1925, an imposing testimony to his fame. The old description of him as 'the Father of Railways' is not exact: yet it still indicates, better than any other, the position he occupies, unchallengeable and unique. Here is a man from north-eastern England whose name is honoured all over the world.

The work he undertook developed fast, far beyond what he himself imagined: through his son Robert—an engineer almost as great as himself—and through men he disapproved of or disliked, such as Brunel and Locke. The railway became caught up in financial activities, of wider and wider scope. These too he condemned, withdrawing from George Hudson in consequence of them. When he died in 1848 the railway was already an established national institution, carried much further in Britain than anywhere else in Europe. The development of the system over the past 150 years is the main theme of the Museum. One comes away from it thinking of course of George Stephenson, but also of the scores of other men who helped that development forward, down to the present day: from Thomas Edmondson and the presses he invented for stamping and printing tickets to Gresley and Stanier and their locomotives. The system has been a co-operative achievement between those who planned and devised it and those who have used what they created ever since, adapting and adding to it. The Museum is a monument to the large community of British railwaymen, of all types and of all grades in that service. It is itself a notable achievement of co-operation, in planning and management; the first national museum in England to be established outside London.

Appendix

The National Railway Collection
as on 1 April 1980

NOTES

ScM Science Museum
NRM National Railway Museum
* Remains of original–much rebuilt – and full size reproduction
† Being restored

Items shown as located at NRM are not necessarily on display and
may be either in the Peter Allen building, on temporary loan to other Museums
or Preservation sites or undergoing restoration at BREL Workshops.

THE NATIONAL RAILWAY COLLECTION
Locomotives: steam

DATE BUILT	OWNER	DESCRIPTION	NO	NAME	LOCATION
1813	Wylam Colliery	0-4-0		*Puffing Billy*	ScM
1822	Hetton Colliery	0-4-0			Beamish
1825	Stockton & Darlington Rly	0-4-0	1	*Locomotion*	Darlington North Road Station Museum
1829	Shutt End	0-4-0		*Agenoria*	NRM
1829	Liverpool & Manchester Rly	0-2-2		*Rocket**	ScM
1829	Liverpool & Manchester Rly	0-4-0		*Sans Pareil*	ScM
1829		0-2-2		*Novelty*	ScM
1837	GWR	2-2-2		*North Star* (Replica)	Swindon
1845	Stockton & Darlington Rly	0-6-0	25	*Derwent*	Darlington North Road Station Museum
1845	LNWR	2-2-2	(49)	(*Columbine*)	NRM
1846	Furness Rly	0-4-0	3	*Coppernob*	NRM
1847	LNWR	2-2-2	173	*Cornwall*	Severn Valley Rly
1857	Wantage Tramway	0-4-0WT	5	*Shannon*	Didcot
1865	LNWR	0-4-0ST		*Pet*	Tywyn
1865	LNWR	0-4-0ST	1439		Shugborough
1866	MR	2-4-0	158A		Midland Rly Trust†
1868	S.Devon Rly	0-4-0T	151	*Tiny*	Dart Valley Rly
1869	NER	2-2-4T	66	*Aerolite*	NRM
1870	GNR	4-2-2	1		NRM

Date	Railway	Wheel arrangement	Number	Name	Location
1874	LSWR	2-4-0WT	298		Dart Valley Rly
1874	Hebburn Works	0-4-0ST	2	*Bauxite*	ScM
1874	NER	0-6-0	1275		Darlington North Road Station Museum
1875	NER	2-4-0	910		NRM
1880	LBSCR	0-6-0T	82	*Boxhill*	NRM
1882	LBSCR	0-4-2	214	*Gladstone*	NRM
1885	NER	2-4-0	1463		Darlington North Road Station Museum
1886	Manchester, Bury, Rochdale & Oldham Tramways	0-4-0	84	(Tram engine)	Dinting
1887	LYR	0-4-0ST		*Wren*	NRM
1889	LYR	2-4-2T	1008		NRM
1892	LNWR	2-4-0	790	*Hardwicke*	NRM
1893	Shropshire & Montgomeryshire Rly	0-4-2T		*Gazelle*	NRM
1893	LSWR	4-4-0	563		NRM
1893	NER	4-4-0	1621		NRM
1894	GER	2-4-0	490		NRM
1897	LSWR	0-4-4T	245		NRM
1897	GWR	0-6-0	2516		Swindon
1897	TVR	0-6-2T	28		Caerphilly
1898	GNR	4-4-2	990	*Henry Oakley*	NRM†
1899	MR	4-2-2	673		Midland Rly Trust
1899	LSWR	4-4-0	120		NRM
1901	SECR	4-4-0	737		NRM
1902	MR	4-4-0	1000		NRM

Locomotives: steam – continued

DATE BUILT	OWNER	DESCRIPTION	NO	NAME	LOCATION
1902	GNR	4-4-2	251		NRM
1903	GWR	4-4-0	3717	City of Truro	Swindon
1904	GER	0-6-0T	87		NRM
1905	GER	0-6-0	1217		Bressingham
1905	GWR	2-8-0	2818		NRM
1907	GWR	4-6-0	4003	Lode Star	Swindon
1909	LTSR	4-4-2T	80	Thundersley	Bressingham
1911	GCR	2-8-0	102		Dinting
1919	NER	0-8-0	901		North Yorkshire Moors Rly
1920	GCR	4-4-0	506	Butler Henderson	Main Line Steam Trust, Loughborough
1921	LNWR	0-8-0	485		Ironbridge
1922	NSR	0-6-2T	2		Shugborough
1923	GWR	4-6-0	4073	Caerphilly Castle	ScM
1924	LMSR	0-6-0	4027		Midland Rly Trust
1925	SR	4-6-0	E777	Sir Lamiel	Hull†
1926	SR	4-6-0	E850	Lord Nelson	Carnforth
1926	LMSR	2-6-0	2700		NRM†
1927	GWR	4-6-0	6000	King George V	Bulmers Hereford
1934	SR	4-4-0	925	Cheltenham	NRM
1934	LMSR	2-6-4T	2500		Bressingham
1934	LMSR	4-6-0	5000		Severn Valley Rly

1936	LNER	2-6-2	4771	*Green Arrow*	NRM
1938	LNER	4-6-2	4468	*Mallard*	NRM
1942	SR	0-6-0	C1		Bluebell Railway
1945	SR	4-6-2	34051	*Winston Churchill*	Didcot
1947	GWR	0-6-0PT	9400		Swindon
1948	SR	4-6-2	35029	*Ellerman Lines* (sectioned)	NRM
1951	BR	4-6-2	70013	*Oliver Cromwell*	Bressingham
1956	Imperial Paper Mills	0-4-0F	1		NRM
1960	BR	2-10-0	92220	*Evening Star*	NRM
1979	BR	0-2-2		*Rocket* (reproduction)	NRM

Locomotives: Electric

1890	C&SL	Bo	No. 1		ScM
1898	Waterloo & City	Bo	75s		NRM
1904	NER	Bo-Bo	1		NRM
1917	NSR	Bo	2		Shugborough
1951	BR	Bo-Bo	26020		NRM
1958	BR	Bo-Bo	E5001		NRM

Locomotives: Diesel

1937	Yorkshire Water Authority	4 Wh		(built by Ruston & Hornsby)	NRM 2ft gauge
1955	BR	Co-Co		*Deltic Prototype*	ScM
1958	BR	A-1-A-A-1-A	D5500		North Yorkshire Moors R
1960	BR	0-6-0	03090		NRM
1960	BR	0-4-0	D2860		NRM
1963	BR	C-C	D1023	*Western Fusilier*	NRM

DATE BUILT	OWNER	DESCRIPTION	NO	LOCATION
Rolling Stock: Powered Units				
1904	NER	Motor Parcels Van	3267	Monkwearmouth
1915	LNWR	Motor 3rd Open	M28249	NRM
1925	SR	Motor	S8143S	NRM
1929	LPTB	Tube Stock	3327	ScM
1934	GWR	Diesel Car	4	NRM
1937	SR	Motor Saloon Brake 2nd	S11179S	NRM
1937	SR	Motor Brake 2nd ⎫ 2	S12123S	Preston Park
1937	SR	Driving Trailer ⎬ BIL	S10656S	Preston Park
		Compo ⎭		
1972	BR	APT-E		NRM
Rolling Stock: Freight				
1797	Peak Forest Canal	Quarry Truck		NRM
1816	Grantham Canal	Tramway Truck		NRM
c.1826		Chaldron Wagon		NRM
1828		Dandy Cart		NRM
		Chaldron Wagon		NRM
		Chaldron Wagon		NRM
c.1850	South Hetton Colliery	Chaldron Wagon	1155	NRM
c.1870	Seaham Harbour (Londonderry) Rly	Chaldron Wagon	31	NRM

Year	Company	Description	Number	Location
1889	Shell-Mex BP	Oil Tank Wagon	512	NRM
1894	LSWR	Brake Van	99	NRM
1895	LSWR	Open Carriage Truck	5830	NRM
1902	NER	20-ton Hopper Wagon		NRM
1912	LBSCR	Open Wagon	3537	NRM
		Sand Wagon	DE14974	NRM
	GNR	8-ton Van	E432764	NRM
1914	GWR	Shunters Truck	W94988	NRM
1916	GWR	Goods Brake Van	53518	NRM
1919	GWR	Hydra D	42193	Didcot
	MR	8-ton Open Wagon		NRM
	GCR	Van		NRM
	LNWR	Van		NRM
	NER	Van		NRM
1922	LBSCR	Cattle Truck	7116	Haven St I.O.W.
1928	ICI	Nitric Acid Tank Wagon	14	NRM
	LMS	Van		NRM
	LNE	Fitted Tube Wagon	181358	NRM
1931	GWR	Goods Van Mink G	112884	NRM
	Stanton Iron Works	12-ton Mineral Wagon		NRM
1935	GWR	Motor Car Van	126438	NRM
1936	SR	Bogie Goods Brake Van		NRM
1936	LMS	3 Plank Fitted Open	472867	NRM
1936	LMS	Tube Wagon	499254	NRM
1936	LNER	20-ton Goods Brake Van	LDE187774	NRM

DATE BUILT	OWNER	DESCRIPTION	NO	LOCATION
1938	LMS	Single Bolster Wagon	722702	NRM
1940	WD	50 War Flat	W161042	NRM
1944	LMS	Lowmac MO	M700728	NRM
1944	GWR	13-ton Open Wagon	DW143698	NRM
1946	SNCF	16-ton Mineral Wagon	ADB192437	NRM
1946	LNER	20-ton Hopper Wagon	E270919	NRM
1949	BR	40-ton Flatrol MHH	B900402	NRM
1950	BR	24-ton Iron Ore Hopper	B436275	NRM
1950	BR	20-ton Weltrol MC	900805	NRM
1950	BR	12-ton Cattle Wagon	B892156	NRM
1951	BR	8-ton Cattle Wagon	B893343	NRM
1951	ICI	Liquid Chlorine Tank Wagon	47484	NRM
1951	BR	Cattle Van (SCV)	S3733S	NRM
1952	BR	30-ton Bogie Bolster Wagon	B943139	NRM
1954	BR	27-ton Iron Ore Tippler	B383560	NRM
1954		National Benzole Oil Tank Wagon	2022	NRM
		Open 13-ton Wagon	W108246	NRM
1955		All steel 16-ton Mineral Wagon	B234830	NRM

1955	BR	All steel 16-ton Mineral Wagon	B227009	NRM
1957	BR	Horse Box (HB)	s96369	NRM
1959	BR	Conflat	B737725	NRM
1960	BR	Banana Van	B882593	NRM
1962	BR	Speedfreight Container	BA4324B	NRM

Rolling Stock: Passenger

Date	Railway	Description	Number	Location
1834		1st		Liverpool
1834		3rd		Liverpool
1834	Liverpool & Manchester Rly	1st } Replicas		Tyseley
1834		3rd }		Tyseley
1834		1st		NRM
1834		3rd		NRM
1834	Bodmin & Wadebridge Rly	2nd		NRM
1834		3rd		NRM
1834		1st & 2nd Composite		NRM
1839	Grand Junction Rly	TPO—on wagon frame		NRM–replica built 1938
1842	London & Birmingham Rly	Queen Adelaide's Saloon	2	NRM
1845	Stockton & Darlington Rly	1st & 2nd composite	59	NRM
1846		1st & 2nd composite	31	Darlington North Road Station Museum
1850		3rd	179	Beamish
1851	Eastern Counties Rly	4-wheel 1st		Bressingham
1861	NBR	Dandy Car (Port Carlisle)	1	NRM
1869	LNWR	Queen Victoria's Saloon	(LMS802)	NRM

Rolling Stock: Passenger – continued

DATE BUILT	OWNER	DESCRIPTION	NO	LOCATION
1872	NLR	Directors' Saloon	1032	NRM
1885	WCJS	Postal Sorting Van	186	NRM
1885	MR	6-wheel Coach	901	NRM
1887	GNR	Brake Van (Passenger)	948	NRM
1887	GWR	6-wheel tri-composite	820	Bristol
1898	ECJS	3rd Corridor	12	NRM
1899	–	Duke of Sutherland's Saloon	57A	NRM
1900	LNWR	Dining Saloon	(LMS76)	NRM
1903	LNWR	King Edward's Saloon	(LMS800)	NRM
1903	LNWR	Queen Alexandra's Saloon	(LMS801)	NRM
1903	LSWR	Tri-composite	3598	NRM
1905	LNWR	Corridor first brake S	LMS5155 and 5154	NRM
1908	ECJS	Royal Saloons	395 and 396	NRM Bressingham
1908	ECJS	Passenger Brake Van	LNE109	NRM
1913	Pullman Car Co	First-class Parlour Car	*Topaz*	NRM
1914	Midland	Dining Car	3463	NRM
1927	LMSR	3rd Open	8207	NRM
1928	LMS	3rd Sleeping Car	14241	NRM

Year	Company	Description	Number	Location
1930	GWR	Composite Dining Car	9605	NRM
1934	GWR	Buffet Car	9631	Severn Valley Rly
1936	CIWL	Sleeping Car	3792	NRM
1937	SR	Buffet Car	S12529S	Nene Valley Rly
1937	LNER	Buffet Car	9135	NRM
1937	LMS	Corridor 3rd Brake	5987	NRM
1939	SR	Travelling Post Office	4920	Nene Valley Rly
1941	LMS	Royal Saloons	798 and 799	NRM
1949	BR	TPO	M30272M	NRM
1955	BR	Non-corridor lavatory composite	E43046	North Yorkshire Moors Rly
1956	BR	TSO (E4286)	NRM75	NRM
1960	BR	Griddle Car	SC1100	NRM
1960	BR	Pullman Kitchen 1st (name *Eagle*)	E311E	NRM
1960	BR	Pullman Parlour 1st (name *Emerald*)	E326E	NRM

Rolling Stock: Departmental

Year	Company	Description	Number	Location
1850	GNR	4-Wheel Hand Crane	112	NRM
?		Match Truck	DE942114	NRM
c.1890	GN	Loco Tender	1002	NRM
1891	NER	Snow Plough	DE900566	NRM
1899	GWR	Hand Crane	537	NRM
1904	MR	Officers' Saloon	2234	NRM

Rolling Stock: Departmental – continued

DATE BUILT	OWNER	DESCRIPTION	NO	LOCATION
1906	NER	Dynamometer Car	902502	NRM
1907	NER	Steam Breakdown Crane	CME13	North Yorkshire Moors Rly
1907	LNWR	Match Truck	LMS284235	Carnforth
1908	LNWR	Steam Breakdown Crane	2987	Carnforth
1926	LNER	Match Truck	DE320952	North Yorkshire Moors Rly
1931/2	LNER	Platelayers' Powered Trolley (petrol)	960209	NRM
1932	LMS	Ballast Plough Brake	197266	NRM
1938	LMS	Mobile Test Unit No. 1	45053	NRM
1949	LMS/BR	Dynamometer Car No. 3	45049	NRM
	BR	Matisa Tamping Machine	741007	NRM

Index

Note: the **bold** numbers refer to the illustrations between pages 40 and 41.

Printed in England for Her Majesty's Stationery Office by
Ebenezer Baylis & Son Ltd., The Trinity Press, Worcester, and London.
Dd 687549 K44 2/81